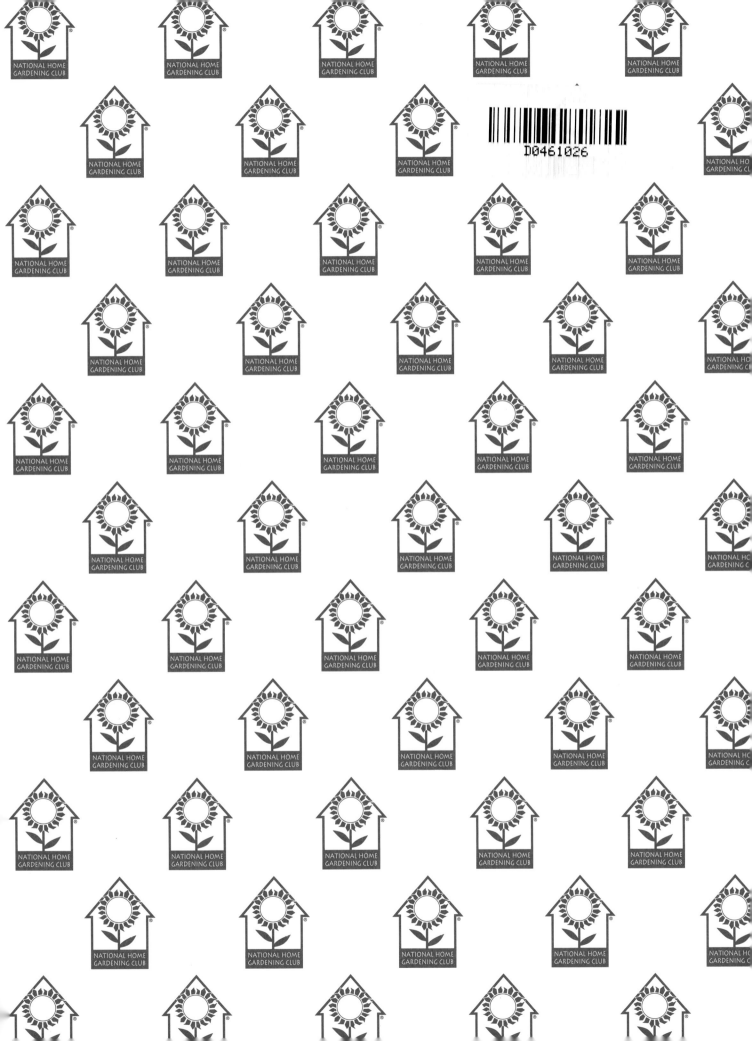

The Gardener's
Butterfly Book

The Gardener's BUTTERFLY Book

A GUIDE TO IDENTIFYING, UNDERSTANDING AND ATTRACTING GARDEN BUTTERFLIES

by Alan Branhagen

NATIONAL HOME
GARDENING CLUB

National Home Gardening Club
Minnetonka, Minnesota

ABOUT THE AUTHOR

Alan Branhagen captured his first butterfly at age 4 and has loved them ever since. An all-around naturalist, he observes and entertains butterflies and other wildlife at his 80- x 120-foot lot in a small town outside Kansas City, Missouri. Over 60 species of butterflies have visited his 2-year-old garden. Alan has traveled widely throughout the country visiting both gardens and natural areas while observing and photographing nature. He has both a Bachelor's and a Master's degree in Landscape Architecture. Alan is Director of Horticulture at Kansas City's famous Powell Gardens, which hosts the nation's most highly attended butterfly festival each August.

PHOTO CREDITS

David Cavagnaro pp.: cover, 10(3), 16-17, 20, 21, 26, 38, 46, 50, 52, 53, 56, 69, 70, 72, 104, 105, 128, 148, 149, 150, 151 both, 152, 162, 164, 169; ©**John Netherton/Animals, Animals** pp.: 2-3; ©**Patti Murray/Animals, Animals** pp.: 8-9, 61, 100-101, 122-123, 147, 184-185; **Bill Beatty** pp: 10, 29, 49(2), 54 both, 55, 57(2), 60 both, 62, 102, 103 both, 106, 114, 124, 137, 141, 142, 143, 146(2), 163, 173, 174, 176, 186, 187, 198, 199(2); ©**Thomas Boyden** pp.: 10, 19, 23, 25, 37, 40-41, 63, 70, 73, 86, 87, 126, 135, 159, 167; **Richard Day/Daybreak Imagery** pp.: 11, 13, 42-43, 58-59, 62, 68, 71, 76(2), 77, 84, 93, 126, 130, 139, 145, 154, 155, 164, 170, 171, 176, 177, 186, 202; **Alan Branhagen** pp.: 18-19, 28, 32, 34, 36, 44; **Paul A. Opler/Nature Photography** pp.: 22, 24, 27, 31, 52, 66, 75, 90, 91, 95, 97, 110, 111 both, 112, 118 all, 119, 134, 135(3), 146, 152, 156, 157, 178, 189, 195, 198, 200(2), 201 all, 202(2), 203(3); **NHGC Archive** pp.: 27, 31, 45 all, 51; **David Ahrenholz** pp.: 30, 99, 115, 186; **Kathy Adams Clark/KAC Productions** pp.: 33, 74, 76, 78, 92, 96, 125, 127, 138, 144, 160, 168 both, 172, 180, 181, 183, 192, 193, 198; **John and Gloria Tveten/KAC Productions** pp.: 33, 74, 78, 82, 94, 106, 107, 108, 109, 116 both, 117, 119, 121(2), 129, 132, 133, 134, 136, 138, 140 both, 165, 179, 188 both, 192, 194 both, 197, 199(2), 200, 204 both, 205; **Jacalyn Goetz** pp.: 35, 56, 57, 65, 68, 85, 88 both, 89, 92, 98, 108, 113, 144, 158, 160, 161, 180, 182, 191; **Bill Johnson** pp: 39, 47 both, 48 all, 49, 50, 51, 64, 86, 107, 109, 162, 193, 196; **Bruce Coleman, Inc.:** ©**Larry West** pp. 41, 79, 119; ©**Bob and Clara Calhoun** p. 67; ©**Wardene Weisser** pp. 72, 178; ©**John Shaw** pp. 102, 107, 120 both; ©**Alan Blank** pp. 166; ©**James Simon** pp.166; **Jay Cossey** pp.: 64, 124, 150, 153, 172, 174, 175; ©**William Folsom** pp.: 80-81, 83, 112, 117, 131, 182; **Jeffrey Glassberg** pp.: 96, 117, 121, 190, 193, 196, 203; ©**James H. Robinson/Animals, Animals** pp.: 104; **Evi Buckner/Nature Photography** pp.: 110, 134, 182.

The Gardener's Butterfly Book

Printed in 2005.

Tom Carpenter
Creative Director

Jenya Prosmitsky
Book Design & Production

Michele Teigen
Senior Book Development Coordinator

Gina Germ
Photo Editor

5 6 7 8 9 / 09 08 07 06 05
ISBN 1-58159-099-7
©2001 National Home Gardening Club

National Home Gardening Club
12301 Whitewater Drive
Minnetonka, MN 55343
www.gardeningclub.com

Contents

CHAPTER 5
Gossamers

CHAPTER 6
Brushfoots

CHAPTER 4
Whites & Sulphurs

CHAPTER 7
Skippers

INTRODUCTION

*B*efore diving into the beautiful world of butterflies, it's important to take a few minutes to understand the creatures better. The pages labeled "Metamorphosis!", immediately following, present the fascinating life cycle of a butterfly, from egg to caterpillar to chrysalis to beautiful winged creature. It's a rare treat to see this process start to finish! Then we'll show you how this book works so that you can get the most out of it now, and for years to come.

Metamorphosis!

Butterflies are insects—six-legged creatures with their skeletons on the outside of their bodies (called an exoskeleton). They are remarkable in how they transform almost magically and miraculously from egg to adult. No other animal goes through such drastic changes. Butterflies go through a complete metamorphosis, meaning they change through all four life stages that insects can morph through: egg, larva, pupa and adult. Butterflies are different from most insects in that they have scaled wings. Only moths share this trait with them (*Lepidoptera*).

Butterflies differ from moths in several ways: Butterflies are active during the day while most moths are active at night. Butterflies generally rest with their wings closed over their backs (except when basking), while most moths rest with their wings open. Butterflies' antennae are club-tipped and never feather-like or thread-like as are moths' antennae. Butterflies pupate as a suspended chrysalis and only some skippers weave somewhat of a cocoon around their pupa. Most moths pupate in a silken cocoon or without any suspension, on or under the ground.

1-EGG ▲

The egg of the butterfly is not unlike that of the bird. A hard shell contains the germ of the future caterpillar, surrounded by the liquid nourishment it needs until it is fully developed and hatches. No incubation or parental care is provided to the egg—it's solely on its own and vulnerable to a myriad of miniature predators. Mother butterfly usually deposits her eggs singly on or near the host plant from which the caterpillar eats and lives. Butterfly eggs require 4 to 10 days to hatch. Most butterflies lay between 100 and 400 eggs, though a few species can lay more than 1,000 eggs.

2-CATERPILLAR (larva) ▲

This is the phase of the butterfly that truly eats in order to grow in size and weight. Its sole mission is to feed without being fed upon. Only a specific plant or group of plants is suitable for each species of caterpillar, and these plants are called its host plants. Most caterpillars have evolved ways to survive and even utilize to their benefit the chemicals that plants use to defend themselves against such herbivorous (plant-eating) creatures. The Monarch is a well-known example of a butterfly that contains the toxic compounds of the milkweed in its body to make it unpalatable to certain bird and mammal predators. These predators learn to avoid butterflies with the Monarch's coloration. Caterpillars generally live about a week to 10 days, though many species spend the winter in a dormant state, rolled up in a leaf.

3-CHRYSALIS (pupa) ▶

The chrysalis is the stage of transformation from caterpillar to butterfly. The chrysalis is often cryptic—leaf-like or twig-like—to hide from would-be predators. Some species, especially the poisonous ones, are bizarrely colored, with highlights of silver and gold! The chrysalis' insides liquify and completely rearrange to become an adult butterfly. Butterflies emerge from the chrysalis in as short a time as a week or as long as six years, waiting for suitable weather to cause them to emerge. Many chrysalises hibernate over winter.

4-BUTTERFLY (imago) ▼

The butterfly is the adult winged stage, whose primary role in life is to reproduce and transport the species to new locations. The wings are there for transportation, escape from predators (by both flight and camouflage) and mate attraction. The small scales that cover the wings and rub off by human touch as if they were dust are colored by pigments or by grooves that refract light. Pigmented scales fade over time and give older butterflies a duller look. Grooved scales do not fade over time; the color we see is not in the scale but is the reflected light. Grooved scales are the iridescent blues on most butterflies. The patterns and colors of the wings' scales are what make butterflies so beautiful. Most live only a few days to two weeks. But some species can live six months, and a few of those that hibernate can live at least 11 months.

BUTTERFLY
C O L O R S

It is noteworthy that a particular butterfly species may look different depending on the seasonal brood from which it is born. Warm-season, cool-season, wet-season and dry-season forms of many species are notable, and it is hard to imagine that they are all the same thing and that their offspring will be of a different form depending on the season. There are no smallish goldfinch-yellow spring Eastern Tiger Swallowtails to hatch from overwintering chrysalises without their big, ochre-yellow summer parents, who themselves are children of the spring ... and no beautiful lavender-edged, orange fall Question Marks to overwinter without orange-and-black summer Question Marks to carry on the species.

BODY PARTS OF A BUTTERFLY

FOREWING

ANTENNAE

HEAD

PROBOSCIS

THORAX

EYES

ABDOMEN

HIND WING

How The Gardener's Butterfly Book Works

Most butterfly reference books are an encyclopedic grouping of information about the butterflies of a particular region. (Boring!) They show a picture or illustration of a butterfly and maybe one of its many forms or races. Similar common butterflies and rare, habitat-restricted butterflies may all be jammed together in a confusing plate for you to visually identify. (Still boring!) But this book takes a different and user-friendly path, displaying beautiful color photographs of the real thing in a garden (not some mounted museum specimen), providing tips on how to attract it, and outlining (in plain English and with more great photos) all the details on that particular lovely creature:

RANGE MAP
- butterfly is resident
- butterfly may colonize or stray
- butterfly sighting is rare

COMMON NAME ————

LATIN NAME ————

DETAILED ESSAY ————

GARDEN HABIT ————

GARDEN NECTAR PLANTS ————

GARDEN HOST PLANTS ————

STATUS ————

HABITAT ————

Giant Swallowtail

Papilio cresphontes

The Latin name describes this swallowtail well, as Crestephonte was one of the Herculids who claimed to be a descendant of Hercules of Greek mythology. Giant Swallowtail is the disputed largest butterfly in North America; the Two-Tailed Swallowtail in the Rocky Mountains and some Eastern Tiger Swallowtails in Florida are

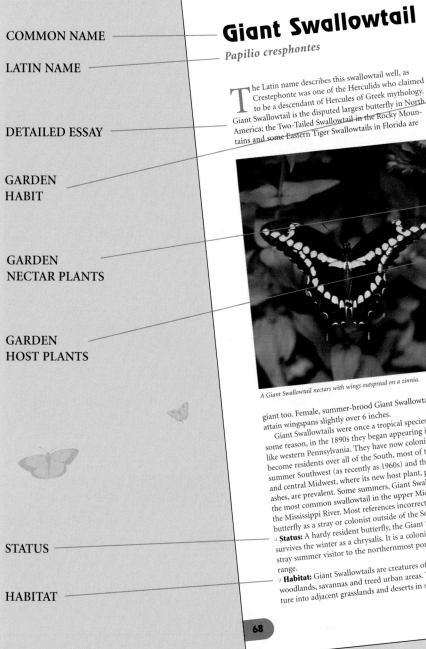

A Giant Swallowtail nectars with wings outspread on a zinnia.

giant too. Female, summer-brood Giant Swallowtails often attain wingspans slightly over 6 inches.

Giant Swallowtails were once a tropical species but, for some reason, in the 1890s they began appearing in places like western Pennsylvania. They have now colonized and become residents over all of the South, most of the hot-summer Southwest (as recently as 1960s) and the South and central Midwest, where its new host plant, prickly-ashes, are prevalent. Some summers, Giant Swallowtails are the most common swallowtail in the upper Midwest near the Mississippi River. Most references incorrectly treat this butterfly as a stray or colonist outside of the South.

□ **Status:** A hardy resident butterfly, the Giant Swallowtail survives the winter as a chrysalis. It is a colonist or irregular stray summer visitor to the northernmost portion of its range.

□ **Habitat:** Giant Swallowtails are creatures of forests, woodlands, savannas and treed urban areas. They will venture into adjacent grasslands and deserts in search of nec-

tar. They are common in gardens and seem to love all the neotropical annual flowers that we have imported from their presettlement homelands.

□ **Garden Habit:** Giant Swallowtails flutter continually while nectaring, their upper wings touching at their lower base while their hind wings are held outspread. They appear a very confusing blur to a predator, and the brown spot in the yellow "X" of their forewing gives them a menacing facial look. This butterfly is readily sought by birds and is often ragged from close calls. Their hyper habits make them best observed and photographed when they are basking in sunshine or puddling on muddy shores or roadsides.

□ **Garden Nectar Plants:** shrubs: butterfly bush, bougainvillea, native azaleas; perennials: swamp milkweed, wild bergamot, lyre-leaf sage, ironweeds; biennials: native thistles, dame's rocket; annuals: pentas, tithonia, *Verbena bonariensis*, zinnias.

□ **Garden Host Plants:** trees: plants in the citrus family; small trees: citrus, hardy orange, hoptrees, prickly-ash, Hercules' club, wild lyme, sea amyris; perennials: gas plant, garden rue. This butterfly also loves orange-jasmine, which is commonly used as a northern houseplant or summer patio plant.

The caterpillar of the Giant Swallowtail looks like a bird dropping.

The Gardener's Butterfly Book

68

IDENTIFICATION   CATERPILLAR   CHRYSALIS

ATTRACTING
TIPS

TIPS
TO ATTRACT

This butterfly can't resist two tropical annuals: If you plant Mexican sunflower and *Verbena bonariensis* you are almost assured of a visit by this swallowtail in hot-summer regions. If you want them to colonize your yard, their all-time-favorite host plants are prickly-ashes found in the South, Southwest and Midwest. Unfortunately, prickly-ashes aren't considered the most ornamental of shrubs or small trees, so plant one in that back corner of your butterfly reserve!

Identification: 4 to 6.25 inches. Unmistakably large, Giant Swallowtails are an overall rich brown with yellow bands that form an "X" in the outer forewing. These swallowtails have an easily visible yellow spot in them.

Caterpillar: A living bird dropping all its life, with a fresh, wet look. This coloration deters birds from eating it. They exude bright-red osmeteria when disturbed. Giant Swallowtails are often called orange dogs in citrus country, where they can become a pest, and colonies are purposely eradicated in citrus country.

Chrysalis: Giant Swallowtail's chrysalis is cryptic brown or gray to look like a stub on the stem or trunk where they form.

A side view of a Giant Swallowtail nectaring on a zinnia.

Swallowtails

69

Red-Spotted Purples, Viceroys, Tawny and Hackberry Emperors flock to a butterfly feeder stocked with a slice of watermelon.

The 120 butterflies you are most likely to encounter in your garden anywhere in the United States and Canada are described in *The Gardener's Butterfly Book*. In one season you can expect about 40 species of butterflies in your garden, whether you're in southern Canada or Florida. A few places—where different gardening regions meet and also near the Mexican border—may attract as many as 60 species. Butterflies restricted to mountain meadows, native deserts, undisturbed prairies, inaccessible wetlands and deep forests are generally not included in this book because you will rarely, if ever, see them in your garden. But it is still important to know that there are such habitat-restricted butterflies and that we need to do our part to protect and manage the habitat which they need to live day to day and for generations to come.

Butterfly Gardening Regions

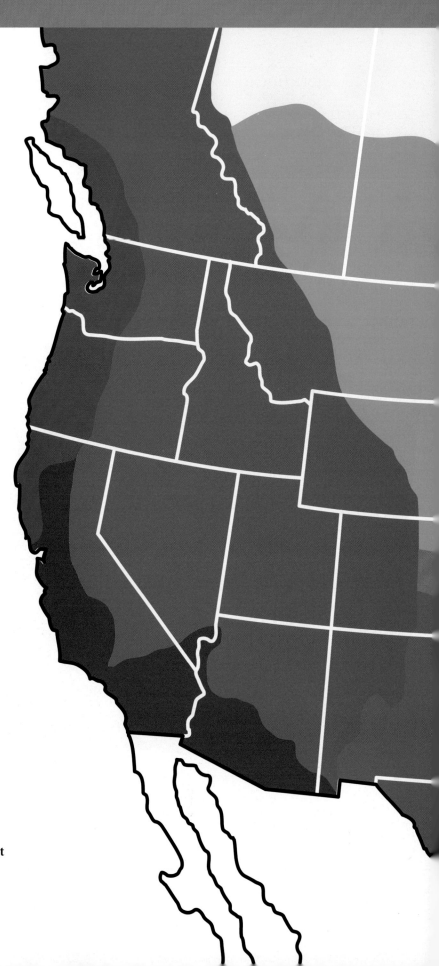

The United States and Canada are divided into 12 "life zones" and gardening regions based on similar gardening practices and butterfly ranges. The zones are defined by areas with similar summer weather; most plants and butterflies are more adapted to these conditions than to minimum winter temperatures. Only the Semitropical Zone of south Texas and south Florida is really defined by its lack of infrequent freezing winter weather. Surprisingly, some adult butterflies overwinter in all regions despite severe cold—they may become active on mild winter days even in the cold Canadian and Rocky Mountain Zones.

The value of these 12 zones is that most zone maps deal with winter's minimal temperature, but actual precipitation, summer heat and length of the growing season are more appropriate to consider when butterflies are the subject. For instance, USDA winter hardiness Zone 8 in central California is quite different from other Zone 8 regions like west Texas, along the Puget Sound of Washington, or along the Atlantic coast of South Carolina. These regions vary greatly in their gardening practices and butterfly population ... and the butterfly gardening regions noted here reflect those differences.

Chapter 1 (starting on page 16) will explore each of these butterfly garden regions in more detail. Of course, you'll find important information there regarding the region where you live and garden ... but it's also interesting to know what goes on elsewhere in the butterfly world.

Pacific Northwest
Mediterranean California
Sonoran
Rocky Mountain-Intermountain
Chihuahuan
Southern Great Plains
Northern Great Plains
Semitropical Florida & Texas
Deep South
Upper South & Lower Midwest
Upper Midwest, Appalachia & Northeast
Northwoods & Canada

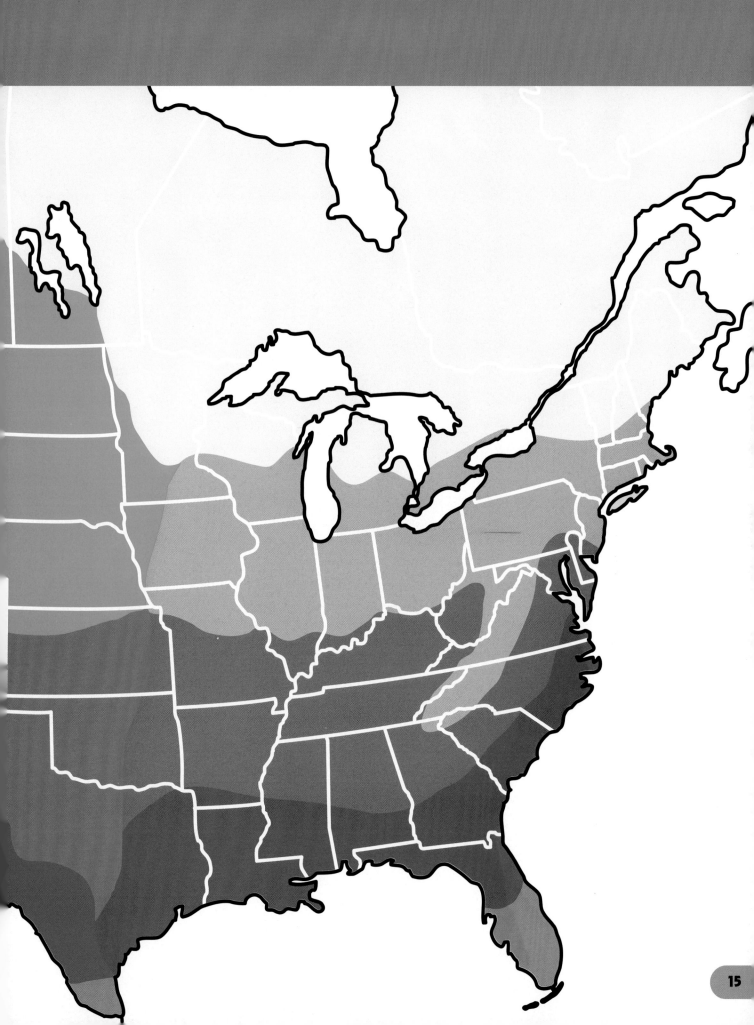

BUTTERFLY GARDENING REGIONS

*T*he United States and Canada are divided into 12 distinct butterfly regions. Of course, the lines separating these regions don't magically represent abrupt and absolute habitat changes. But the regions do, in general, represent zones where you will find certain types of butterflies using the available habitat in particular kinds of ways. If you ever travel to these regions, you'll know which butterflies to look for. And as a home gardener, it's important to know which butterflies reside in your area, and can be attracted to your yard, garden and plantings. In that respect, you'll find no shortage of ideas and plant suggestions here!

Pacific Northwest

The Pacific Northwest is an area of mild, dry summers and mild winters of heavy rainfall and cloud cover. Highest elevations receive heavy snowfall. Cool springs and falls create a gardener's paradise. Some coastal areas receive very little warmth in summer, while the Willamette, Umpqua and Rogue Valleys have relatively warm, dry summers. This cool, wet, forested climate is not friendly to most butterflies, so this region has the lowest diversity of butterflies in North America. The region's vegetation is composed of coniferous forests dominated by temperate rain forests of Sitka spruce and western hemlock in northern coastal areas, and evergreen redwood forests from Brookings, Oregon, south. Mostly evergreen forests of western hemlock accompanied by western redcedar, red alder and Douglas fir dominate the Strait of Georgia, Puget Sound, Coast Ranges and the windward west side of the Cascade Ranges. The Willamette Valley is dominated by open woodlands and savannas of Oregon white oak and Douglas fir and is now a premier agricultural region. The warm summer Umpqua and Rogue River Valleys are dominated by woodlands and savannas of Douglas fir, ponderosa pine, Oregon white oak and California black oak. Mixed coniferous/evergreen forests and woodlands inhabit the Siskiyou Mountains and inland areas of northwest California and are dominated by Douglas fir, sugar pine, white fir, California black oak, California-laurel, Oregon white

A botanical garden along the coast of Oregon. Many butterfly attracting plants are located between its sheltering hedges.

oak and tan oak. Subalpine woodlands and meadows of mountain hemlock, subalpine fir and Pacific silver fir occur on the highest elevations of the Olympic Mountains and with this region's interface with the Rocky Mountain/Intermountain Zones.

The butterflies inclusive of the region's major urban areas and described in this reference include: Anise Swallowtail, Western Tiger Swallowtail, Pale Swallowtail, Western White, Cabbage White, Pacific (Sara) Orangetip, Clouded Sulphur, Orange Sulphur, Purplish Copper, Western Tailed-Blue, Spring Azure, Silvery Blue, Brown Elfin, Hydaspe Fritillary, Pacific Fritillary, Mylitta Crescent, Variable Checkerspot, Satyr Comma, Mourning Cloak, Milbert's Tortoiseshell, California Tortoiseshell, Painted Lady, West Coast Lady, Red Admiral, Lorquin's Admiral, Common Ringlet, Common Wood-Nymph, Monarch, Silver-

A Painted Lady.

Spotted Skipper, Dreamy Duskywing, Two-Banded Checkered-Skipper, Woodland Skipper and Dun Skipper.

The best butterfly nectar plants for the garden in this region include: evergreen tree: golden chinkapin; shrubs: butterfly bush, bluemist spirea, mock orange, shrubby cinquefoil, garden lilacs, blueberries, abelia, escallonia, evergreen huckleberry; perennials: pearly everlasting, golden marguerite, common milkweed, Cascade aster, New York asters, basket-of-gold, fireweed, ox-eye and Shasta daisies, mountain thistle, Indian thistle, coreopsis, golden and cut-leaved daisy (fleabanes), sulphur wild buckwheat, sneezeweed, elecampane, perennial sweet pea, lavender, common horehound, selfheal, orange coneflower, arrowleaf groundsel (ragwort), alfalfa, red clover, white clover, verbenas, hairy vetch; annuals: globe amaranth, Dyer's woad, edging lobelia, globe gilia, marigolds, Mexican sunflower, pansies, violas, zinnias.

The best butterfly host plants for the garden in this region include: shade trees: quaking aspen, Oregon white oak, California black oak, black locust; small trees: black hawthorn, bitter cherry, Cascara buckthorn; shrubs: Saskatoon serviceberry, deerbrush, red-twig dogwood, red-flowering currant, ocean-spray, Hooker's willow and Scouler's willow, wild lilacs (mountain-balm, buckbrush, blueblossom wild lilacs); vine: wisteria; perennials: hollyhocks, pearly everlasting, pussytoes, globe thistle, sweet fennel, checker-mallows, alfalfa, red and white clover, violets; annuals: bloodflower, parsley, dill, carrots, nasturtiums, cleome, pansies, violas.

REGIONAL BUTTERFLY GARDENING
TIPS

Butterfly gardening tips must stress the need for sheltered south-facing sites, open to the sun, which create a warm microclimate for most butterflies to be active and nectar in. A ridge or hilltop opening in the forest or wooded urban area, or even in open country, is an ideal butterfly garden site as butterflies seek out these spaces when searching for a mate. This is called hilltopping. Butterflies are active from March in early spring through November in late fall. Nectar plants and water can be important to attract butterflies during the height of the midsummer drought.

Western Garden Book Climate Zones: #3 of the Coast Ranges, all of 4, 5, 6 and Zones 15 and 17 north of San Francisco Bay. USDA winter hardiness Zones 7, 8, 9 and 10.

Mediterranean California

Mediterranean California is considered the perfect climate for human habitation, with warm, dry summers (hot in the Central Valley) and moist, mild winters. Frosts are infrequent and snowfall is generally rare. Coastal areas receive very few hot summer days and can be in the same summer heat zones as the Canadian climate region. It's a land of periodic droughts that can last for years until an El Niño brings abundant and flooding rains. The Mediterranean California landscape is green with the cool-season grasses of winter and becomes a beautiful golden color with the onset of summer's drought—one of the reasons California is called the Golden State. The fog, soils, elevation and mountains create immensely variable gardening conditions, often specific to a small region—consult your local gardening experts. The diversity of butterflies is rich and varied, with many local endemic species. Most species are restricted to specific remnants of native habitat.

The region's natural vegetation varies from grasslands and shrubby chaparral to oak and pine savanna and woodlands. Chaparral is the main plant community, dominated by large and small evergreen shrubs, including chamise, several manzanitas, various wild lilacs and scrub oaks. In regions that are slightly cooler and more moist the chaparral gives way to some of the most beautiful oak woodlands or savannas in the world. Magnificent specimens of evergreen and deciduous oaks comprise pastoral scenes among grasslands rich in butterflies. Foothills may include digger and Coulter pines (south), both of which have huge, heavily armored cones. Higher elevations that ring the Central Valley begin to transition into the Rocky Mountain/Intermountain Zone of coniferous forests but are dominated by the Jeffrey pine, which is unique to the region. Here also is where the largest trees on earth, the Giant sequoias, grow

An oak savanna filled with wildflowers and flanked by mountains is typical natural habitat in Mediterranean California.

on the west slopes of the central Sierra Nevadas. Coastal areas harbor gargantuan, gnarly old Monterey cypresses, which grow wild in just a few coastal areas but have been planted along the entire coastline naturally made up of chaparral and Bishop pines. Redwoods reside in some of the fog-shrouded coastal valleys but they have more in common with the Pacific Northwest gardening region. The hot, dry Central Valley was occupied mainly by grassland and now comprises the richest agricultural area in the world. The Central Valley and its prairie-esque landscape has the fewest butterflies of any part of this particular region.

Butterflies found in gardens in the Mediterranean region and covered in this book are as follows: [The interior Central Valley may not contain some of these species; and (n) signifies those prevalent in the northern portion, (s) signifies those in the southern portion of the region, (e) signifies the eastern portion, (w) signifies the western portion, and (c) signifies the central portion. There are many regional endemic species and subspecies confined to unique habitats, from dunes to mountain range meadows. Many of these localized butterflies are among the most endangered animals in North America—and one of them, the Xerces Blue, is the only North American butterfly driven to extinction.] Pipevine Swallowtail, Anise Swallowtail, Western Tiger Swallowtail, Pale Swallowtail, Checkered White, Cabbage White, Pacific (Sara) Orangetip, Orange Sulphur, California Dogface, Southern Dogface (s), Cloudless Sulphur (s), Sleepy Orange (s), Dainty Sulphur, Purplish Copper, Great Purple Hairstreak, California Hairstreak, Hedgerow Hairstreak, Thicket Hairstreak, Brown Elfin, Western Pygmy-Blue, Marine Blue, Ceraunus Blue (s), Reakirt's Blue, Eastern Tailed-Blue (n), Western Tailed-Blue, Spring Azure, Silvery Blue, Acmon Blue, Lupine Blue, Mormon Metalmark (n), American Snout (s), Gulf Fritillary, Variegated Fritillary, Callippe Fritillary, Hydaspe Fritillary (n), Field Crescent (n), Mylitta Crescent, Variable Checkerspot, Satyr Comma, Mourning Cloak, Milbert's Tortoiseshell, American Lady, California Tortoiseshell, Painted Lady, West Coast Lady, Red Admiral, Common Buckeye, Lorquin's Admiral, California Sister, Common (California) Ringlet, Common Wood-Nymph (n), Great Basin Wood-Nymph, Monarch, Queen (s), Silver-Spotted Skipper, Northern Cloudywing, Funereal Duskywing, Common Checkered-Skipper (n), White Checkered-Skipper (s), Common Sooty-Wing, Orange Skipperling (s), Fiery Skipper, Juba Skipper, Western Branded Skipper, Sachem, Sandhill Skipper, Woodland Skipper, Umber Skipper, Eufala Skipper.

The best butterfly nectar plants for the garden in this region include: evergreen trees: Pacific madrone, manzani-

A California Sister.

tas; small trees: acacias, chamise, California buckeye, blue palo verde, desert-willow, citrus, summer-holly, lemonadeberry, sugarbush, California-laurel, chastetrees; shrubs: abelias, Shaw's century plant, manzanitas, wild lilacs, claret-cup cactus, escallonia, evergreen huckleberry, toyon, lantanas, mahonias, coffeeberry, butterfly bushes, bluemist spirea, whitethorn, coyote brush, red-twig dogwood, apache-plume, chuparosa, calliandras, lantanas, mock oranges, cape plumbago (vine-like), currants, sages, garden lilacs; perennials: yarrow, wild onions, snapdragons, columbines, thrift, milkweeds, asters, brodiaeas, Jupiter's beard, leadwort, blue dicks, ox-eye daisy, coreopsis, wild buckwheats, Pacific iris, blazingstars, deerweed lotus, lupines, bergamots, coyote mint, oregano, California coneflower, salvias, California goldenrod, Triteleias, *Verbena bonariensis*; biennials: fleabanes, wallflowers; annuals: bur marigolds, cosmos, gaillardias, purple butterfly mint, phacelia, marigolds, Mexican sunflower, pansies, violas, zinnias.

The best butterfly host plants for the garden in this region include: shade trees: California black oak, California sycamore, Fremont and black cottonwoods; evergreen trees: California live oak, canyon live oak; small trees: netleaf hackberry, Pacific willow, toyon, scrub oak; shrubs: sennas, California lilacs, hibiscus, bush lupines, mistletoe, oceanspray, coffeeberry, currants, arroyo willow; vines: California pipevine, passionvines, wisterias; perennials: hollyhocks, snapdragons, milkweeds, asters, wild buckwheats, cudweed, wild sunflowers, deerweed lotus, lupines, monkeyflowers, penstemons, checkermallows, nasturtiums, violets; biennials: artichoke, foxgloves, fennel; annuals: bloodflower, pansies, violets.

REGIONAL BUTTERFLY GARDENING
TIPS

Butterflies are present and active in gardens all year. Be sure to provide sunny, sheltered microclimates for them in winter and all year in cool coastal areas (especially in summer!). Garden with native plants and those native to other Mediterranean climates that are adapted to the region's drought-filled summers, to conserve scarce water resources. Be sure to provide nectar plants and a wet stone or puddle during summer's drought.

Western Garden Book Climate Zones 7, 8, 9, 14, 16, 18, 19, 20, 21, 22, 23, 24 and Zones 15 and 17 south of San Francisco Bay. USDA winter hardiness Zones 8, 9 and 10.

Sonoran

The Sonoran region is known for its deserts. Winter rains may cause floriferous springs when the desert is abloom with ephemeral annual wildflowers and alive with butterflies. Summers are *very* hot during the day, with cool nights, and bring patchy monsoonal rains, which give the region the other half of its rainfall. Winters are mild and nearly frost-free in the subtropical desert of the lower Colorado and Gila river basins. Winter is much colder in the Mojave and other high-desert areas. Mild daytime highs become frosty nights in high-desert regions as well. The region is known for its high winds and in higher regions its late spring frosts. The most unusual portion of this region is the mountainous southeastern corner of Arizona and the southwestern corner of New Mexico, which is actually in its own unique zone, associated with Mexico—often called the Madrean region. There are many unique butterflies here and nowhere else (just as with birds). Other mountain ranges in this region transition to pinyon-

The Sonoran Desert outside Tucson, Arizona.

juniper woodlands and contain refuges of coniferous forest and even alpine areas on and near their summits, with butterflies and gardening more in common with the Rocky Mountains. The dominant plant of this region is the creosote bush, which grows in an almost evenly spaced pattern across the desert, with bare ground in between. Most of the wildflowers are annual and bloom, fruit and die in those short periods of moist, favorable conditions—the bare ground provides a perfect flower bed for them. Cacti and succulents also are associates to this region and they survive by accumulating reserves of water in their fleshy leaves or stems. Many plants are summer or drought deciduous.

A Pipevine Swallowtail.

Some unique distinctive plants of this region are the giant tree-like Saguaro cactus (not hardy in high deserts like the Mohave), ocotillo, Joshua tree and other smaller-trunked yuccas, century plant and palo verde trees. The lower Colorado and other rivers provide riparian habitat now sadly choked in alien tamarisk brush but still containing cottonwoods, willows, desert-willow and, in a few cases, the California fan palm. In eastern portions of the region the desert transitions into semidesert grasslands and oak savannas of Emory oak with some characteristics of the Chihuahuan region.

Butterflies found through most of the region and described in this book include: Pipevine Swallowtail, Black Swallowtail, Giant Swallowtail, Checkered White, Cabbage White, Southwestern (Sara) Orangetip, Desert Orangetip, Orange Sulphur, Southern Dogface, Cloudless Sulphur, Mexican Yellow, Sleepy Orange, Dainty Sulphur, Great Purple Hairstreak, Gray Hairstreak, Western Pygmy-Blue, Marine Blue, Ceraunus Blue, Reakirt's Blue, Spring Azure, Fatal Metalmark, Palmer's Metalmark, American Snout, Gulf Fritillary, Variegated Fritillary, Bordered Patch, Texan Crescent, Phaon Crescent, Mylitta Crescent, Variable Checkerspot, Mourning Cloak, Red Admiral, American Lady, West Coast Lady, Common Buckeye, Viceroy, California Sister, Monarch, Queen, Funereal Duskywing, White Checkered-Skipper, Common Sooty-Wing, Orange

Skipperling, Fiery Skipper, Sachem, Eufala Skipper. Many unique Mexican species are found along the border region but are so limited in distribution that they are not covered by this book.

The best butterfly nectar plants for the garden in this region include: evergreen trees: saguaro; small trees: acacias, blue palo verde, desert-willow, ocotillo, goldenball leadtree, mesquite; shrubs: Shaw's century plant, beebush, red barberry, woolly butterfly bush, Mexican bird of paradise, rabbitbrush, littleleaf cordia, claret-cup cactus, desert-lavender, lantanas, Texas sage, littleleaf sumac, sugarbush, Dorri sage, autumn sage, ajamete, seepwillow, desert broom, pink fairyduster, condalias, bush dalea, brittlebush, kidneywoods, apache-plume, chuparosa; perennials: desert marigold, Jupiter's beard, frogfruit, verbenas, southwestern vervain, Mexican plumbago, goldeneyes, dwarf white zinnia; annuals: Mexican sunflower, zinnias.

The best butterfly host plants for the garden in this region include: shade tree: Fremont cottonwood; evergreen tree: Arizona white oak, Emory oak; small trees: acacias, netleaf hackberry, citrus, mesquites, New Mexico locust; shrubs: ajamete, seepwillow, calliandra, spiny hackberry, mistletoe, fern acacia, indigobush, kidneywoods, coyote willow; vines: pipevines, passionvines; perennials: milkweeds, sideoats grama, desert senna, wild sunflowers, frogfruit, mallows, globe mallows; biennials: fennel, parsley; annuals: bloodflower, sunflowers, snapdragons.

REGIONAL BUTTERFLY GARDENING
TIPS

Butterflies are present year-round but peak in March to November. Garden with those plants adapted to the dry desert conditions of this region to conserve its precious water resources. The canopy of a tree—even a small tree—helps provide a warm microclimate to shelter butterflies during cold nights. Windbreak plantings, buildings and fences are important to block the region's high winds and provide a protected respite for butterflies.

Western Garden Book Climate Zones 11, 12, 13 and Zone 10 west of and including the southwest corner of New Mexico. USDA winter hardiness Zones 8, 9, 10.

Rocky Mountain-Intermountain

The Rocky Mountain-Intermountain region's hot, dry summers are a boon to butterflies. Higher elevations have short, warm summers and at the highest elevations frosts can occur on any night of the year and a surprising number of butterflies are adapted to such harsh conditions. Winter is long and cold—especially in the mountains. Protective, reliable snowcover combined with well-drained soils improves the hardiness of many plants that would otherwise be killed by winter lows. The Columbia and Snake River Valleys are the mildest, as is lowland western Nevada. Chinook winds and arctic fronts can create both warm and cold weather, with drastic temperature changes in a matter of hours. Early and late frosts are prevalent—creating unique gardening opportunities. Winter snowfall provides most of the region's water, so intermountain valleys are lush only along river and stream floodplains.

The region's habitats vary greatly, from wooded floodplains to desert-like intermountain lowlands of sagebrush and pinyon-juniper woods, foothills of ponderosa pines, coniferous-forested mountains and alpine meadow mountaintops. Aspen groves are a signature plant of mid and high elevations. The short summer season high in the mountains makes the wildflowers bloom all at once—

An autumn view of Rocky Mountain National Park, Colorado: Typical butterfly habitat of this high-mountain region.

contributing to some of the most beautiful butterfly-filled wildflower meadows imaginable. Various rainfall/snowfall patterns are created by the many mountain ranges contributing to the variety of habitats. Butterfly species change from habitat to habitat, so butterfly diversity is quite high, overall.

The following species are seen in most of the inhabited parts of the region and are described in this book. There are many endemic species in unique habitats and many northern species are found in alpine areas.

Anise Swallowtail, Old World Swallowtail, Western Tiger Swallowtail, Pale Swallowtail, Two-Tailed Swallowtail, Checkered White, Western White, Cabbage White, Large Marble, Stella (n) and Southwestern (s) Orangetips, Clouded Sulphur, Orange Sulphur, Dainty Sulphur (s), Purplish Copper, Colorado Hairstreak (s), California Hairstreak, Coral Hairstreak, Hedgerow Hairstreak, Thicket Hairstreak, Juniper Hairstreak, Gray Hairstreak, Western Pygmy-Blue (s), Marine Blue (s), Reakirt's Blue (s), Western Tailed-Blue, Spring Azure, Silvery Blue, Melissa Blue, Lupine Blue, Brown Elfin, Western Pine Elfin, Mormon Metalmark, Variegated Fritillary (s, e), Great Spangled Fritillary, Callippe Fritillary, Hydaspe Fritillary (n), Mormon Fritillary, Field Crescent, Mylitta Crescent, Variable Checkerspot, Hoary Comma, Mourning Cloak, Milbert's Tortoiseshell, California Tortoiseshell, American Lady (s), Painted Lady, West Coast Lady, Red Admiral, Common Buckeye (s), Viceroy, Weidemeyer's Admiral (s2/3), Lorquin's Admiral (n1/3), California Sister (s), Common Ringlet, Common Wood-Nymph, Great Basin Wood-Nymph, Small Wood-Nymph, Monarch, Silver-Spotted Skipper, Northern Cloudywing, Two-Banded Checkered-Skipper (n), Small Checkered-Skipper (s), Common Checkered-Skipper, Common Sooty-Wing, Juba Skipper, Western Branded Skipper, Tawny-Edged Skipper, Woodland Skipper, Dun Skipper (s), Bronze Roadside-Skipper (s).

The best butterfly nectar plants for the garden in this region include: shade tree: lindens; small trees: apples, wild plums; shrubs: indigobush, butterfly bush, wild

A Two-Tailed Swallowtail.

lilacs, rabbitbrush, feather dalea, cliff fendlerbush, wild mock orange, potentilla, antelope bitterbush, garden lilacs; perennials: yarrows, pussytoes, golden marguerite, milkweeds, asters, Jupiter's beard, daisies, purple coneflowers, wild buckwheats, woolly sunflower, gaillardias, western blueflag, lavenders, blazingstars, horehound, mountain monardella, scabiosas, threadleaf groundsel (ragwort), showy goldeneye, violets; biennial: dame's rocket; annuals: marigolds, verbenas and *Verbena bonariensis*, pansies, violas, zinnias.

The best butterfly host plants for the garden in this region include: shade trees: Gambel oak, quaking aspen, narrowleaf cottonwood, green ash, black locust; evergreen trees: Rocky Mountain juniper, ponderosa pine; small trees: New Mexico locust, wild plums; shrubs: Fendler's wild lilac, indigobush, rocksprays, sumacs, golden currant, squaw currant, gooseberries, willows; perennials: hollyhocks, pussytoes, rock cresses, artemisias, milkweeds, grama grasses, Indian paintbrushes, poppy-mallows, prairie-clovers, wild buckwheats, lupines, penstemons, alfalfa, violets; annuals: dill, fennel, parsley, snapdragons, pansies, violas.

REGIONAL BUTTERFLY GARDENING
TIPS

Butterflies are active from April or May through September or October depending on the elevation. Gardening with early and late frosts is a must and at higher elevations plants must be frost tolerant—plant cool-season plants or southern winter annuals! Native plants and those from similar continental mountainous climates are quite well adapted. Be sure to provide nectar during summer droughts and provide a wet stone or puddle for butterflies to drink from—summer humidity is often low, contributing to a butterfly's moisture needs. As with other western zones, water is a critical gardening factor and xeriscaping with drought-tolerant plants is essential.

Western Garden Book Climate Zones 1, 2, 3 (except Coast Ranges). USDA winter hardiness Zones 3 and 4 up high and Zones 5 and 6 most inhabited.

Chihuahuan

The Chihuahuan region receives most of its rainfall in late summer and fall. The moist landscape responds with heavy flowering, which corresponds with maximum butterfly emigration and abundance. Spring rains following winter moisture can also bring an abundance of wildflowers. It is a high-desert to shortgrass grassland, with cold to mild winters and very hot summers. As with similar low-humidity climates, hot days are followed by cool nights and cold nights can rebound into mild days. It is an area of very quick changes in weather, and temperatures in winter may drop to near zero following an arctic "blue northern" front. Late frosts are prevalent and freezing weather can occur into April.

This region is also dominated by the creosote bush, with

Open scrubby woodlands, desert and dry grasslands typify the cold-wintered, Chihuahuan landscape.

The Gardener's Butterfly Book

mesquite trees also prevalent—especially in overgrazed areas. Open pinyon-juniper woodlands blanket higher elevations, with a few small islands of Rocky Mountain coniferous forest on the highest elevations. Succulent agaves, yuccas and many species of cold-hardy cacti are prevalent and well adapted to the dry, windy landscape. Riparian floodplain areas along rivers and streams support cottonwoods, willows and desert-willow. Unfortunately, the weedy tamarisk shrub has choked out much of the riparian space for native plant diversity, which threatens the abundance of butterflies that rely on the obliterated nectar and host plants.

Prevalent butterflies found throughout most of the region and described by this book (those with * are some local specialties related to butterflies described) include: Pipevine Swallowtail, Black Swallowtail, Giant Swallowtail, Two-Tailed Swallowtail, Checkered White, Cabbage White, Clouded Sulphur, Orange Sulphur, Southern Dogface, Cloudless Sulphur, Lyside Sulphur*, Mexican Yellow, Sleepy Orange, Dainty Sulphur, Great Purple Hairstreak, Juniper

Annual phlox makes an excellent butterfly nectar source.

Hairstreak, Gray Hairstreak, Western Pygmy-Blue, Marine Blue, Reakirt's Blue, Lupine Blue, American Snout, Gulf Fritillary, Variegated Fritillary, Dotted Checkerspot*, Fulvia Checkerspot*, Bordered Patch, Vesta Crescent*, Phaon Crescent, Pearl Crescent, Painted Crescent, Question Mark, Mourning Cloak, American Lady, Painted Lady, Red Admiral, Common Buckeye, Hackberry Emperor, Red Satyr*, Monarch, Queen, Funereal Duskywing, Common Checkered-Skipper, Common Sooty-Wing, Orange Skipperling, Fiery Skipper, Sachem, Bronze Roadside-Skipper, Nysa Roadside-Skipper, Dotted Roadside-Skipper*.

The best butterfly nectar plants for the garden in this region include: shade tree: western soapberry; evergreen tree: Texas madrone; small trees: Roehmer acacia, catclaw acacia, desert-willow, goldenball leadtree, mesquite, mimosa, wild plum; shrubs: century plant, claret-cup cactus, Texas sage, shrub acanthus, willow baccharis, red barberry, desert wild lilac, Fendler's wild lilac, ocotillo, catclaw mimosa, common cholla, autumn sage, Wright's beebrush

A Lupine Blue shows off its exquisite detail.

or high-mass, bird-of-paradise bush, buttonbush, rabbitbrush, condalias, Texas snakewood, kidneywoods, Apache plume, cliff fendlerbush, pink mimosa, Mexican buckeye; perennials: sand verbena, yarrows, huisache daisy, butterflyweed, showy milkweed, Jupiter's beard, babywhite-aster, purple coneflowers, Engelmann daisy, wild buckwheats, blazingstars, cardinal flower, blackfoot daisy, garden phlox, frogfruit, Mexican plumbago, woolly paperflower, sedums, threadleaf groundsel, prairie verbena, plains ironweed, goldeneye; biennial: yellow woolly-white; annuals: starthistle, annual gaillardia, globe amaranth, tansy-aster, sleepy daisy, lemon bergamot, lantanas, Pavonia (shrub in warmest areas), marigolds, Mexican sunflower, zinnias.

The best butterfly host plants for the garden in this region include: shade trees: sugarberry, velvet ash, Rio Grande cottonwood, plains cottonwood, Gambel oak; small trees: Lindheimer hackberry, netleaf hackberry, hoptrees, lime prickly-ash; shrubs: kidneywoods, mistletoe; vines: pipevines, passionvines; perennials: hollyhocks, asters, milkweeds, grama grasses, poppy-mallows, Lindheimer senna, two-leaved senna, daleas and prairie-clovers, globe thistle, wild buckwheats, cudweeds, Mexican plumbago, dusty millers, globe mallows, alfalfa; biennials: Texas thistle, fennel, parsley; annuals: snapdragons, bloodflower, kale, cleome, ornamental cotton, annual phlox, marigolds.

Southern Great Plains

The southern Great Plains is the land where extremes are the norm, with intensely hot, windy, dry, long summers and cold, dry winters, with a wild roller-coaster ride of weather from fall through spring. Temperatures may be warm even in winter, followed by severe cold fronts. Late-spring freezes can be devastating. Hot, dry summers (humid to dry from east to west) are very favorable to butterflies, which can be quite spectacular, as those from adjacent regions seem to wander willy-nilly here more so than in any other region.

The original vegetation varies from tallgrass prairie of big bluestem, Indian grass, tridens and switchgrass in the east to midgrass (mixed) prairie and shortgrass prairie of buffalograss and various grama grasses on the western edge. Prairie areas are rich in prairie forbs (the wildflowers) with something always in bloom from spring through fall. Bands of forest follow stream corridors and various hilly regions westward. Floodplain forests of cottonwood, wil-

A view of Konza Prairie, Kansas, shows typical natural butterfly habitat of the Southern Great Plains.

lows, sugarberry, hackberry, elm and ash, give rise to rich bottomland terraces of bur oak, pecan and black walnut. Upland woodlands and savannas of post oak, blackjack oak, eastern redcedar and eastern redbud are open and full of wildflowers.

Common butterflies found and described in this book include (those with * are some local specialties related to butterflies described): Pipevine Swallowtail, Black Swallowtail, Giant Swallowtail, Eastern Tiger Swallowtail, Checkered White, Cabbage White, Clouded Sulphur, Orange Sulphur, Southern Dogface, Cloudless Sulphur, Mexican Yellow, Soapberry Hairstreak*, Coral Hairstreak, Juniper Hairstreak, Gray Hairstreak, Western Pygmy-Blue, Marine Blue, Reakirt's Blue, Summer Azure, Eastern Tailed-Blue, Melissa Blue, Gulf Fritillary (s, e), Variegated Fritillary, Fulvia Checkerspot*, Gorgone Checkerspot*, Texan Crescent, Vesta Crescent*, Phaon Crescent, Pearl Crescent, Mourning Cloak, American Lady, Painted Lady, Red Admiral, American Snout, Common Buckeye, Red-Spotted Purple, Viceroy, Hackberry Emperor, Tawny Emperor, Little Wood Satyr, Common Wood-Nymph, Monarch, Queen, Silver-Spotted Skipper, Funereal Dusky-wing, Hayhurst's Scallopwing, Common Checkered-Skipper, Common Sooty-Wing, Common Least Skipper, Orange Skipperling, Fiery Skipper, Eufala Skipper, Satchem, Delaware Skipper, Nysa Roadside-Skipper, Common Roadside-Skipper, Dusted Skipper*.

The best butterfly nectar plants for the garden in this region include: shade tree: western soapberry; small trees: gum bumelia, mesquite, roughleaf dogwood, wild plum, sumacs, rusty blackhaw viburnum; shrubs: butterfly bush, Chicksaw plum, buttonbush; perennials: sand verbena, yarrows, anise hyssop, huisache daisy, chives, butterflyweed, showy milkweed, asters, Jupiter's beard, wavy-leaf thistle, chrysanthemums, Engelmann daisy, dotted blazingstar,

American Snout—a Southern Great Plains butterfly.

cardinal flower, garden phlox, sedums, prairie verbena, ironweeds; biennial: Texas thistle; annuals: starflower, sleepy daisy, cosmos, annual gaillardia, globe amaranth, tansy aster, lemon bergamot, pavonia, annual phlox, marigolds, Mexican sunflower, verbenas, vinca, zinnias.

The best butterfly host plants for the garden in this region include: shade trees: sugarberry, hackberry, green ash, cottonwood, black cherry, black locust, western soapberry; evergreen tree: eastern redcedar; small trees: netleaf hackberry, roughleaf dogwood, hoptree, wild plums; shrubs: sumacs (smooth, shining, skunkbush), willows; vines: Dutchman's pipe, passionvines; perennials: hollyhocks, pussytoes, native asters, milk-vetches, fennel, native milkweeds, grama grasses, poppy-mallows, river oats, prairie clovers, wild licorice, wild sennas, alfalfa, frogfruit, globe mallows, tridens, violets, flax; biennial: native thistles; annuals: bloodflower, flowering kale, partridge pea, ornamental cotton, parsley, dill, dusty miller, snapdragons.

Northern Great Plains

The northern Great Plains are another region where extremes are the norm but the extremes are definitely on the cold side. Summers are short, but warm to hot—a lot more heat than the Canadian, Rocky Mountain and Pacific Northwest regions. A hot-summer dry spell is a regular occurrence. Snowfall can occur from November through March, and winters can be brutally cold—at least -20°F— with severe windchill. Warm chinook winds bring periodic mild winter days to the western edge of the region. The northern portion of the region has relatively low humidity but the southern edge of the region can be hot and humid in summer and influenced by the Gulf of Mexico.

Tallgrass prairie dominates the landscape in the east—now prime farmland—changing to mid-grass prairie, then short-grass prairie and ranchland in the dry western edge of the region. Eastern deciduous forest fingers westward along many of the major streams and their protected valleys—floodplain forests of cottonwood, willow, ash, silver maple, hackberry and elm harbor lots of butterflies and some additional eastern species. The region interfaces with the Rocky Mountains in the west and groves of Ponderosa pine creating pine savannas on the prairie. These habitats will have some of the butterflies of the Rocky Mountains. The northern interface with the Canadian region's northwoods has groves of aspen, spruce and jack pine (often called the "parkland") and has northwoods butterfly species likewise.

Common butterflies found in this region include: Black Swallowtail (s), Anise Swallowtail (n, c), Old World Swallowtail (n, c), Eastern Tiger Swallowtail (s), Canadian Tiger Swallowtail (n, c), Checkered White, Western White, Cabbage White, Clouded Sulphur, Orange Sulphur, Mexican Yellow (s), Dainty Sulphur (s), Bronze Copper, Purplish Copper, Coral Hairstreak, Striped Hairstreak, Gray Hairstreak,

A prairie in the Northern Great Plains. Note the fire-scorched birch tree and woodland backdrop.

The Gardener's Butterfly Book

Snapdragons are host plants for the beautiful Common Buckeye butterfly.

A Callippe Fritillary.

gumweed, western wallflower, Joe-Pye-weeds, blazingstars, goldenrods, arrowheads, clovers, prairie verbena; biennials: native thistles, dame's rocket, black-eyed Susans; annuals: butterfly bush, globe amaranth, marigolds, *Verbena bonariensis*, zinnias.

The best butterfly host plants for the garden in this region include: shade trees: hackberry, green ash, quaking aspen; evergreen trees: white spruce, jack pine, ponderosa pine, eastern white pine; small trees: American plum, chokecherry; shrubs: sand cherry, smooth sumac, clove currant, willows; perennials: rock cresses, artemisias, asters, milk-vetches, hollyhocks, milkweeds, pussytoes, grama grasses, alfalfa, violets, bush-clovers; biennials: black-eyed Susan, native thistles; annuals: parsley, dill, fennel, dusty miller, snapdragon, cockscomb.

Reakirt's Blue (s), Eastern Tailed-Blue (s), Western Tailed-Blue (n, c), Spring Azure, Summer Azure, Silvery Blue, Melissa Blue, Lupine Blue (w), Variegated Fritillary, Great Spangled Fritillary, Aphrodite Fritillary, Regal Fritillary (s), Edward's Fritillary (c, w), Callippe Fritillary (n, c), Meadow Fritillary (n, e), Silvery Checkerspot (s), Pearl Crescent, Question Mark (s), Eastern Comma (e), Gray Comma, Mourning Cloak, Milbert's Tortoiseshell, American Lady (s, e), Painted Lady, Red Admiral, Common Buckeye (s), Viceroy, Red-Spotted Purple (s), White Admiral (n), Hackberry Emperor (s), Little Wood Satyr (s), Common Ringlet, Common Wood-Nymph, Monarch, Silver-Spotted Skipper, Northern Cloudywing, Common Checkered-Skipper, Common Sooty-Wing (s), Common Least Skipper (s, e), Peck's Skipper, Tawny-Edged Skipper, Delaware Skipper, Dun Skipper, Common Roadside-Skipper.

The best butterfly nectar plants for the garden in this region include: shade tree: Basswood; small trees: American plum, Canada plum; shrubs: red-twig dogwood, willows, common lilac; perennials: yarrow, chives, butterflyweed and native milkweeds, asters, wavy-leaf thistle, ox-eye daisy,

REGIONAL BUTTERFLY GARDENING
TIPS

Butterflies are active from April into October. The wind that sweeps across the northern Great Plains should be blocked or baffled for a top-notch butterfly garden. Respect the region's cold winters and plant hardy plants! Butterflybush makes a great container plant here but must be overwintered in a garage or basement, or be replanted as an annual each year. Many fabulous prairie wildflowers are underutilized or untested, and many of the regions shrubs are underappreciated. Short, warm-to-hot summers are excellent for growing most annuals and just one planting will last the whole growing season. In choosing many native perennials, it is important to get your stock from local sources—especially in the northern half of this region. Big bluestem purchased from Illinois, for example, will not set seed in Manitoba because the season is too short; but big bluestem from local stock does just fine.

USDA winter hardiness Zones 3 and 4.

Semitropical Florida & Texas

Hot and humid south Texas and Florida share butterflies of tropical affinities not found elsewhere. Rainfall peaks between late summer and early fall in south Texas, and south Florida has a wet-season (May to October) dry-season pattern. This region can regularly have frost-free winters, though winters can occasionally have severe freezes, especially in central Florida and Texas. The winter of 1983-84 was particularly devastating to central Florida and to the lower Rio Grande Valley of Texas, when most exotic palms and citrus were killed. Key West, Florida, has never recorded a frost. Butterflies are present year-round in good numbers in this region. The lower Rio Grande Valley of Texas has the greatest butterfly diversity in the United States and Canada—nearly 90 species found nowhere else! It is physically connected to the American tropics, which has more species of butterflies than the rest of North America, Europe, Asia, Africa and Australia combined. There are so many species in south Texas (265) that only the dominant ones are listed. South Texas is actually a part of the Tamaulipan desert, filled with thorny scrub growth, including Texas ebony, great lead-tree, several acacias and mesquite with scattered live oaks northward and along the coast. Lush woodlands of Mexican ash, cedar elm, and formerly Texas palmetto grow along the floodplain and resacas (oxbows) of the Rio Grande. South Florida contains many habitats, including southern swamps of bald cypress, pond cypress and swamp red maple; sandy scrub of various oaks and pines—and pinewoods of slash pine; the saw grass marsh expanse called the Everglades; tropical hammocks of live oak, mahogany, strangler figs, gumbo-limbo, papaya, royal palm; mangrove swamps at the wetland ocean and gulf interface, and coconut palms and sea-grape along the dunescape. Hawaii also would fall into this zone but has only 2 species of native butterflies (the Kameamea Lady and Pea Blue) and slightly more than a dozen introduced butterflies, the Asian Xuthus' Swallowtail being most dramatic.

Common butterflies found in the semitropical region include: [those with a (FL) are found only in Florida and those with a (TX) are found only in Texas. Butterflies introduced in Hawaii have a "+" after their name.] Pipevine Swallowtail, Polydamas Swallowtail, Zebra Swallowtail (FL), Black Swallowtail, Giant Swallowtail, Eastern Tiger Swallowtail (FL), Spicebush Swallowtail (FL), Palamedes Swallowtail (FL), Checkered White, Great Southern White, Orange Sulphur, Southern Dogface, Little Sulphur, Barred Yellow, Sleepy Orange, Tailed Orange (TX), Mexican Yellow (TX), Cloudless Sulphur, Orange-Barred Sulphur, Large Orange Sulphur, Lyside Sulphur (TX), Dainty Sulphur, Great Purple Hairstreak, Gray Hairstreak, Red-Banded Hairstreak (FL), Atala (FL), Western Pygmy-Blue+ (TX), Eastern Pygmy-Blue+ (FL), Marine

A forest of palmettos provides habitat for semitropical butterflies.

Blue (TX), Cassius Blue, Ceraunus Blue, Reakirt's Blue (TX), Fatal Metalmark (TX), Little Metalmark (FL), American Snout (TX), Gulf Fritillary+, Zebra, Julia, Variegated Fritillary, Bordered Patch (TX), Pearl Crescent, Phaon Crescent, Texan Crescent (TX), Question Mark (TX), American Lady+, Painted Lady+, Red Admiral+, Common Buckeye, White Peacock, Viceroy, Hackberry Emperor, Empress Leila (TX), Tawny Emperor, Carolina Satyr, Monarch+, Queen, Silver-Spotted Skipper (FL), Long-Tailed Skipper, Horace's Duskywing, Funereal Duskywing (TX), Common Checkered-Skipper (TX), Tropical Checkered-Skipper, Common Sooty-Wing (TX), Hayhurst's Scallopwing (FL), Least Skipper (FL), Orange Skipperling (TX), Dun Skipper, Delaware Skipper (FL), Fiery Skipper+, Whirlabout, Sachem, Eufala Skipper, Ocola Skipper, Clouded Skipper, Brazilian Skipper, Monk Skipper (FL), Nysa Roadside Skipper (TX), Celia's Roadside Skipper (TX).

The best butterfly nectar plants for the garden in this region include: shrubs: buttonbush, glory bower, golden dewdrop, firebush, heliotropes, lantanas, plumbagos; vines: coralvine, bougainvilleas, morning glories, Mexican flame vine; perennials: asters, Texas thistle, shrimp plant, pentas, frogfruit, tropical sage, lyre-leaf sage, porterweeds, ironweeds, verbenas; biennial: thistle; annuals: Spanish needles, vinca, annual phlox, Mexican sunflower, zinnias.

The best butterfly host plants for the garden in this region include: shade tree: sugarberry; evergreen trees: sea amyris, sweetbay magnolia, redbay, live oak; small trees: acacias, citrus, southern bayberry, leadtrees, lime prickly-ash; shrubs: indigobush, pawpaws, candle plant, Christmas senna, spiny hackberry, mistletoe, plumbagos, willows, wild

A Tropical Checkered-Skipper perches on lantana—one of its favorite nectar sources.

coonties; vines: pipevines, balloonvine, passionvines; perennials: bloodflower, asters, water bacopa, Spanish needles, cannas, wild sennas, sweet everlastings, frogfruit, Mexican plumbago, water ruellias; biennials: thistle, dill, fennel, parsley; annuals: Spanish needles, nasturtiums.

Mexican flame vine—a great nectar plant for Semitropical Florida and Texas.

REGIONAL BUTTERFLY GARDENING
TIPS

Butterflies are active year-round. Plant a live oak or other shade tree to shelter both butterflies and some tender plants on cold, frosty nights. An occasional freeze will kill back tropical plants but they usually will regrow from their roots. Visit Butterfly World in Coconut Creek, Florida, and the NABA Butterfly Park next to Bentsen-Rio Grande State Park in Mission, Texas—they are world-class butterfly parks that will help you with many butterfly gardening ideas. The region's humid climate (even in Texas) lessens the moisture needs of butterflies when compared to dry, low-humidity western areas.

USDA winter hardiness Zones 9 and 10.

Deep South

Trees draped in Spanish moss are the symbol of this region of hot, humid summers and mild winters. Rainfall is plentiful year-round and hurricanes can bring torrential rains in late summer and fall. Some butterflies are fairly active all year, as nine months of the year are frost free even though hard freezes occur most winters (El Niño years may be frostless). Butterflies are rich and varied, being second only to semitropical Texas in diversity.

The once-dominant plant community of this region was a vast savanna of long-leaf pine, wiregrass and abundant wildflowers known as flatwoods. Gardens with a canopy of high pines and lush plantings beneath, which mimic this landscape, are ideal for attracting butterflies. Floodplain areas are heavily forested and vary from swamps of bald cypress, swamp red maple, water tupelo and sweetbay magnolia to rich bottomland woods of cherrybark oak, water oak, sweetgum and southern magnolia.

Magnificent wide-spreading live oaks draped in Spanish moss are some of the most fabulous trees anywhere—and remarkably able to withstand hurricane-force winds. Open meadows and wetlands among these rich forests teem with butterflies. The tropical-looking undergrowth of native

Longleaf pine flatwoods comprise the signature natural habitat of the Deep South.

dwarf palmetto in floodplains and saw palmetto in flat-woods is distinctive. Many tropical plants thrive here in the summer but most must be sheltered or brought indoors during winter's short cold snaps.

Common butterflies found in your garden in the Deep South include: Pipevine Swallowtail, Zebra Swallowtail, Black Swallowtail, Giant Swallowtail, Eastern Tiger Swallowtail, Spicebush Swallowtail, Palamedes Swallowtail, Checkered White, Cabbage White, Falcate Orangetip, Orange Sulphur, Southern Dogface, Cloudless Sulphur, Little Yellow, Sleepy Orange, Dainty Sulphur, Little Metalmark, Great Purple Hairstreak, Red-Banded Hairstreak, Banded Hairstreak, Striped Hairstreak, Juniper Hairstreak, Summer Azure, Eastern Tailed-Blue, Cassius Blue, Ceraunus Blue, Henry's Elfin, Eastern Pine Elfin, American Snout, Gulf Fritillary, Variegated Fritillary, Pearl Crescent, Phaon Crescent, Texan Crescent, Question Mark, Eastern Comma, Mourning Cloak, American Lady, Painted Lady, Red Admiral, Common Buckeye, Viceroy, Red-Spotted Purple, Hackberry Emperor, Tawny Emperor, Southern Pearly-Eye, Little Wood Satyr, Carolina Satyr, Common Wood-Nymph, Monarch, Queen, Silver-spotted Skipper, Hoary Edge, Long-Tailed Skipper, Northern Cloudywing, Southern Cloudywing, Confused Cloudywing, Juvenal's Duskywing, Horace's Duskywing, Wild Indigo Duskywing, Common Checkered-Skipper, Common Sooty-Wing, Hayhurst's Scallopwing, Zabulon Skipper, Dun Skipper, Northern Broken-Dash, Tawny-Edged Skipper, Least Skipper, Delaware Skipper, Sachem, Fiery Skipper, Whirlabout, Eufala Skipper, Ocola Skipper, Clouded Skipper, Brazilian Skipper.

The best butterfly nectar plants for the garden in this region include: small trees: mimosa, devil's walkingstick, eastern redbud, wild plums, rusty blackhaw viburnum; shrubs: butterfly bush, buttonbush, native azaleas, blueberries; vines: coralvine, Carolina climbing aster, morning glories; perennials: pussytoes, asters, milkweeds, cannas, mistflower, blazingstars, Turk's turban, pickerelweed, scarlet sage, mealy

A female Cloudless Sulphur alights on a red zinnia.

sage, lyre-leaf sage, goldenrods, stokesia, *Verbena bonariensis*, verbenas, crownbeards, ironweeds, violets; biennials: thistle; annuals: Spanish needles, vinca, lantanas, pentas, annual phlox, porterweeds, marigolds, Mexican sunflower, pansies, violas, zinnias.

The best butterfly host plants for the garden in this region include: shade trees: sugarberry, tulip tree, black cherry, black locust, black oaks, sassafras; evergreen trees: eastern redcedar, sweetbay magnolia, redbay, loblolly pine, live oak; small trees: eastern redbud, southern bayberry, wild plums, hoptree, coastal plain willow; shrubs: indigobush, switchcane, pawpaws, summersweet clethra, rough-leaf dogwood, spicebush, mistletoe, sumacs; vines: Dutchman's pipe, maypop, passionvines, American wisteria; perennials: asters, milkweeds, wild indigos, cannas, wild senna, river oats, sweet everlasting, swamp sunflower, frogfruit, dusty miller; biennials: thistle, fennel, parsley; annuals: snapdragons, bloodflower, Spanish needles, partridge pea, ornamental cotton, pansies, violas.

REGIONAL BUTTERFLY GARDENING
TIPS

Butterflies are most active from March to December but can be observed year-round. Plant a live oak or slash pines for sheltering butterflies on frosty winter nights. Remove Japanese honeysuckle and Chinese privet, which have taken over many suburban wood-lots and choked out native weedy wildflowers and butterfly host plants. Leave a space unmowed for both winter annuals and weedier plants to flower and provide nectar during the winter and early spring. An annual flower border of lantanas, pentas and vinca is sure to bloom through the entire hot summer and provide nectar for clouds of two of the region's most distinctive butterflies: the Cloudless Sulphur and the Gulf Fritillary—and many other species as well.

USDA winter hardiness Zones 8 and 9.

Upper South & Lower Midwest

Continually hot, humid summer weather for four to five months with cool to cold winters characterize this zone. Mild Indian summer days are prevalent and full of butterflies. Rainfall is plentiful, with snowfall rarely lasting more than a week on the northern edges and a day on the southern edge. Forest butterflies abound but are most prevalent in openings where wildflowers and weeds proliferate.

The region is the heart of the temperate forest province of eastern North America with a great diversity of trees. Trees grew to immense size along this region's floodplains—especially from the lower Wabash River, lower Ohio and southward into the Mississippi, where cypress swamps were also once prevalent and now are replaced by soybean fields. Poorer-soil upland areas support loblolly and shortleaf pine, oaks and hickories, with tulip trees east of the Mississippi. The region blends into the prairies on its western edge, and most of the Ozarks are an open, flower-filled savanna-like forest. Areas with shallow soils over bedrock—called glades—occur in much of the region and are nature's great butterfly gardens, with spaces open to the sun and lots and lots of nectar-rich flowers from early spring until late fall. Open sandbars along many of the region's forested rivers and creeks are also gathering places

Ozark glades make outstanding butterfly habitat.

for butterflies, where beautiful assemblages of swallowtails puddling are not an uncommon sight. Agriculture has kept many areas open but is the dominant component of the landscape only in the Mississippi floodplain region.

Common butterflies found in the upper South & lower Midwest include: Pipevine Swallowtail, Zebra Swallowtail, Black Swallowtail, Giant Swallowtail, Eastern Tiger Swallowtail, Spicebush Swallowtail, Checkered White, Cabbage White, Falcate Orangetip, Clouded Sulphur, Orange Sulphur, Southern Dogface, Sleepy Orange, Little Yellow, Cloudless Sulphur, Dainty Sulphur (w), Coral Hairstreak, Banded Hairstreak, Striped Hairstreak, Juniper Hairstreak, Gray Hairstreak, Red-Banded Hairstreak, Spring Azure, Summer Azure, Eastern Tailed-Blue, Henry's Elfin, Eastern Pine Elfin, American Snout, Gulf Fritillary (s), Variegated Fritillary, Great Spangled Fritillary, Silvery Checkerspot, Baltimore Checkerspot, Pearl Crescent, Question Mark, Eastern Comma, Mourning Cloak, American Lady, Painted Lady, Red Admiral, Common Buckeye, Viceroy, Red-Spotted Purple, Hackberry Emperor, Tawny Emperor, Common Wood-Nymph, Northern Pearly-Eye, Little Wood-Satyr, Monarch, Silver-Spotted Skipper, Hoary Edge, Northern Cloudywing, Southern Cloudywing, Confused Cloudywing, Juvenal's Duskywing, Horace's Duskywing, Wild Indigo Duskywing, Common Checkered-Skipper, Common Sooty-Wing, Hayhurst's Scallopwing, Swarthy Skipper, Least Skipper, Fiery Skipper, Sachem, Peck's Skipper (n), Tawny-Edged Skipper, Northern Broken-Dash, Dun Skipper, Delaware Skipper, Zabulon Skipper, Clouded Skipper (s), Common Roadside-Skipper.

The best butterfly nectar plants for the garden in this region include: small trees: mimosa, eastern redbud, roughleaf dogwood, apple, wild plums, peach, blackhaw and rusty blackhaw viburnums; shrubs: glossy abelia, butterfly bush, New Jersey tea, buttonbush, summersweet clethra, mock oranges, wild azaleas, garden lilacs; vines: Carolina climbing aster, morning glories; perennials: fragrant hyssop, chives, milkweeds, asters, chrysanthemums, purple coneflowers, mistflower, Joe-Pye-weeds, blazingstars, garden phlox, mountain mints, lyre-leaf sage, cupplant, goldenrods, crownbeards, rose verbena, *Verbena bonariensis*, ironweeds; biennials: thistles, dame's rocket, black-eyed Susans; annuals:

A female Black Swallowtail nectars on a cosmos.

bloodflower, vinca, cosmos, globe amaranth, lantanas, pentas, scarlet sage, mealy sage, porterweeds, marigolds, Mexican sunflower, verbenas, zinnias.

The best butterfly host plants for the garden in this region include: shade trees: sugarberry, hackberry, white ash, tulip tree, black cherry, black oak, black locust, sassafras; evergreen trees: eastern redcedar, shortleaf pine, Virginia pine; small trees: pawpaw, eastern redbud, roughleaf dogwood, sweetbay magnolia, wild plums, hoptree; shrubs: switchcane, New Jersey tea, silky dogwood, spicebush, sumacs, rose acacia, willows, prickly-ash; vines: Dutchman's pipe, passionvines, American wisteria; perennials: pussytoes, asters, milkweeds, Gray's sedge, river oats, gas plant, sweet everlastings, fennel, wild sennas, wild sunflowers, penstemons, violets; biennials: thistles, black-eyed Susans; annuals: snapdragons, bloodflower, cleome, parsley, partridge pea, ornamental cotton, dusty miller, marigolds, pansies, violas.

REGIONAL BUTTERFLY GARDENING
TIPS

Butterflies are generally active here from March through November. Two plants are a must in your garden in this region— each of which hosts four species of butterflies. Choose a hackberry or sugarberry for a beautiful barked shade tree, and plant a border of annual, self-sowing partridge pea, which blooms from midsummer to frost. You will instantly have a colony of eight species of butterflies in your garden. Provide a sunny, sheltered site filled with late-blooming flowers like single chrysanthemums, asters and verbenas that will provide nectar on Indian summer days for late butterflies that have survived a frost. Many woodlots here are threatened or already choked by Japanese honeysuckle, and this plant should be removed to allow space for open-woods grasses and legumes, which host many butterflies.

USDA winter hardiness Zones 5, 6, 7.

Upper Midwest, Appalachia & Northeast

Warm, with occasional hot, humid weather characterizes this zone's summer. Winters are cold with snowcover lasting for three months in the northern portion to only 10 days or so on the southern edge. Rainfall is usually sufficient through the growing season, although periodic dry spells in summer can occur. There are more butterflies in the hotter-summer Midwestern portion of this region, with fewer species unique in the East—this is probably related to the summer's prevailing southwesterly winds, which bring more emigrant butterflies from the butterfly-rich Southwest.

This region is also known as the transition zone because it contains elements of the northwoods, although those from the south predominate. Rich blacksoil tallgrass prairie abloom with many wildflowers once carpeted the western portion of the region, which now comprises more than one-half of the United States' prime farmland. Pockets of prairie once occurred eastward across the whole region to Long Island, and these pockets are especially rich in butterflies. Oak-hickory and floodplain forests traverse the entire region with beech and tulip trees becoming prevalent east of Lake Michigan. There are pockets of northern forests,

Forested riverbanks in Iowa typify the landscape of the Upper Midwest, Appalachia and Northeast.

especially in the mountains and in southern New England.

Common butterflies found in this region include: [(s) southern, (n) northern, (c) central, (e) eastern and (w) western portions of the region.] Pipevine Swallowtail (s, c), Zebra Swallowtail (s, c), Black Swallowtail, Giant Swallowtail (w, c), Eastern Tiger Swallowtail, Spicebush Swallowtail (c, e), Checkered White (w), Cabbage White, Clouded Sulphur, Orange Sulphur, Southern Dogface (w), Little Yellow, Dainty Sulphur (w), Bronze Copper, American Copper, Coral Hairstreak, Banded Hairstreak, Striped Hairstreak, Juniper Hairstreak (e, w), Gray Hairstreak, Spring Azure, Summer Azure, Eastern Tailed-Blue, Brown Elfin (e), Eastern Pine Elfin (e), American Snout, Variegated Fritillary, Great Spangled Fritillary, Regal Fritillary (w, extirpated in the East), Aphrodite Fritillary (n, e), Meadow Fritillary, Silvery Checkerspot, Baltimore Checkerspot, Pearl Crescent, Question Mark, Eastern Comma, Gray Comma, Mourning Cloak, Compton Tortoiseshell (n, e), Milbert's Tortoiseshell, American Lady, Painted Lady, Red Admiral, Common Buckeye, Viceroy, Red-Spotted Purple, Hackberry Butterfly (w, c), Tawny Emperor (w, c), Common Wood-Nymph, Northern Pearly-Eye, Little Wood Satyr, Monarch, Silver-Spotted Skipper, Hoary Edge (e), Northern Cloudywing, Southern Cloudywing, Juvenal's Duskywing, Horace's Duskywing (s), Wild Indigo Duskywing, Common Checkered-Skipper, Common Sooty-Wing, Least Skipper, European Skipper, Fiery Skipper, Sachem (w, c), Peck's Skipper, Tawny-Edged Skipper, Northern Broken-Dash, Dun Skipper, Delaware Skipper, Common Roadside-Skipper.

The best butterfly nectar plants for the garden in this region include: shade tree: basswood; small trees: apples, wild plums; shrubs: New Jersey tea, buttonbush, mock oranges, garden lilacs, blueberries (e), viburnums; perennials: fragrant hyssop, chives, milkweeds, asters, butterfly bush (usually killed back each winter), chrysanthemums, purple coneflowers, Joe-Pye-weeds, wild geranium, blazingstars, Oriental lilies, wild bergamot, garden phlox, pickerelweed, mountain mints, rudbeckias, arrowheads, cupplant, rosinweed, goldenrods (stiff and showy); biennials: dame's rocket, thistles, black-eyed Susans; annuals: bloodflower, cosmos, globe amaranth, lantanas, pentas, marigolds, Mexican sunflower, *Verbena bonariensis*, zinnias.

The Monarch—A common and beautiful resident of this region.

The best butterfly host plants for the garden in this region include: shade trees: yellow birch, hackberry, white ash, tulip tree, black cherry, quaking aspen, black oaks, black locust, sassafras (c, e); evergreen trees: eastern redcedar, jack pine, eastern white pine; small trees: pawpaw (s, c), sweetbay magnolia, wild plums, staghorn sumac, rose acacia; shrubs: New Jersey tea, gray dogwood, red-twig dogwood, spicebush (c, e), smooth sumac, gooseberries, willows, prickly-ash; vines: Dutchman's pipe, hops, Kentucky wisteria; perennials: hollyhocks, pussytoes, asters, milkweeds, wild indigos, Gray's sedge, river oats, turtlehead, prairie clovers, globe thistle, fennel, gas plant, wild sunflowers, bottlebrush grass, alfalfa, violets; biennial: thistles; annuals: cockscomb, snapdragons, bloodflower, partridge pea, cleome, dill, parsley, nasturtiums, dusty miller, marigolds.

REGIONAL BUTTERFLY GARDENING
TIPS

Butterflies are active from April through October, with the peak butterfly flight occuring in late July and early August. Plant flowers from the tallgrass prairie element of this region's flora to really attract droves of butterflies. Butterflyweed, stiff coreopsis, pale and regular purple coneflowers, cupplant, New England asters, frost aster, stiff goldenrod and showy goldenrod are some of the best. A simple border of the following blazingstars—marsh blazingstar, prairie blazingstar, savanna blazingstar—meadow blazingstar and rough blazingstar—will provide continual nectar-rich bloom from July through September! Exotic bush honeysuckles, buckthorns and, in the east, Norway maples have severely degraded many woodlots and shaded out the host plants many butterflies need—please remove these plants from your property! Two of the best spring nectar sources in this zone are late-blooming garden lilacs and an exotic biennial, dame's rocket. Dame's rocket has naturalized over most of the area and is starting to become a pest—deadhead it in your garden and keep it away from pristine natural areas.

USDA winter hardiness Zones 4, 5, 6.

Northwoods & Canada

The Northwoods and Canadian Zone is characterized by its sweet, cool summers with only a few brief heat waves. The growing season doesn't begin until May and ends in September. Summer days are warm, and nights are cool. Many folks enjoy vacation homes, lodges or camps in this zone to escape the heat of summer and play in the region's extensive lakes and wildlands. Fall is distinguished with dazzling fall color brought on by consistent, cool night temperatures. Spring is short, with winter being the longest season, as snowcover can readily last from Thanksgiving to Easter.

The Canadian region is also known as the northwoods, and pines and birches are what first come to mind. The region is actually a split between coniferous evergreens and

This flower-filled Minnesota garden is a sure butterfly attractor.

deciduous trees. Eastern white, red and jack pines dominate in some areas, while sugar maples dominate in others (along with beech and hemlocks from the Great Lakes eastward). Vast groves of aspen and birch can also be found, and spruces, firs and tamarack are found in the coldest, boggiest zones. The butterflies peak in meadows among the forest—some of these meadows are filled with native prairie plants like blue lupine, fireweed and asters, but naturalized meadow flowers such as tall buttercups, orange hawkweed, garden lupines, vetches and ox-eye daisies can really put on a show—with accompanying butterflies. Far northern and eastern Maritime Provinces have the fewest butterflies, but there are more butterflies here than in the Pacific Northwest Zone.

A Purplish Copper.

The butterflies found in gardens in the inhabited parts of the region are: [(w) west, (e) east, * related specialties]: Black Swallowtail, Canadian Tiger Swallowtail, Cabbage White, Clouded Sulphur, Orange Sulphur, Bronze Copper, American Copper, Purplish Copper (w), Coral Hairstreak, Striped Hairstreak, Eastern Pine Elfin, Brown Elfin, Spring Azure, Summer Azure, Eastern Tailed-Blue, Western Tailed-Blue (w, e) Silvery Blue, Great Spangled Fritillary, Aphrodite Fritillary, Meadow Fritillary, Silvery Checkerspot, Baltimore Checkerspot, Northern Crescent, Tawny Crescent (w), Question Mark, Eastern Comma, Green Comma, Gray Comma, Satyr Comma, Mourning Cloak, Compton Tortoiseshell, Milbert's Tortoiseshell, Painted Lady, Red Admiral, Viceroy, White Admiral, Common Wood-Nymph, Northern Pearly-Eye, Little Wood Satyr, Common Ringlet, Monarch, Northern Cloudywing, Dreamy Duskywing*, Arctic Skipper*, European Skipper, Least Skipper, Peck's Skipper, Long Dash, Tawny-Edged

Skipper, Dun Skipper, Common Roadside-Skipper.

The best butterfly nectar plants for the garden in this region include: shade tree: basswood; small trees: apple, wild plums; shrubs: red-twig dogwood, potentilla, red raspberry, willows, meadowsweet, garden lilacs, blueberries, viburnums; perennials: yarrow, anise hyssop, pearly everlasting, pussytoes, milkweeds, asters, coreopsis, ox-eye daisy, purple coneflower, fireweed, Joe-Pye-weed, wild geranium, orange hawkweed, blazingstars, buttercups, arrowheads, golden ragwort, goldenrods, ironweeds; biennials: thistles, dame's rocket, black-eyed Susans; annuals: sweet alyssum, bachelor buttons, sulphur cosmos, globe amaranth, scabiosas, marigolds, verbenas, zinnias.

The best butterfly host plants for the garden in this region include: shade trees: yellow birch, paper birch, quaking aspen; evergreen trees: eastern white pine, jack pine; small trees: wild plums, chokecherry; shrubs: black chokeberry, red-twig dogwood, gooseberry, blueberries; perennials: pussytoes, pearly everlasting, milkweeds, milk-vetches, turtlehead, lupines, grasses, sedges, violets; biennials: thistles, black-eyed Susans; annuals: dill, fennel, parsley, flowering kale, nasturtiums.

REGIONAL BUTTERFLY GARDENING
TIPS

Butterflies are active from May through September and occasionally into early October. Leave weedy places filled with meadow grasses, sheep sorrel, clovers, vetches, hawkweeds and dogbanes unmowed, and likewise leave wet areas of docks and sedges. Make sure to have a woodpile with hibernating spaces for the numerous northwoods butterflies that overwinter here. Locate butterfly gardens in areas with ample solar access, as a cold snap can hit anytime during the growing season, and butterflies will need a place to bask and nectar on cool days.
USDA winter hardiness Zones 2, 3 and 4.

BUTTERFLY GARDENING TIPS

*T*his book will help you identify and understand a wide variety of North American butterflies. But before we do that, let's take some time to investigate what it will take for you to attract these creatures to your garden, lawn and landscape. It's not hard, expensive or time-consuming at all! In this section you'll see how to select a proper site for starting a butterfly garden, prepare soil and design the garden. You'll see which host plants to provide to help attract butterflies, and also how to make habitat butterfly-friendly in general. Finally, we make a few suggestions on how to "tread lightly" with pesticides and lawn care, to make sure your colorful garden butterflies stay safe and healthy, and reproduce more butterfly beauty for you to drink in.

Site Selection

For a butterfly garden, select a site with the best solar access. Butterflies are cold-blooded and require warmth and sunshine. Morning shade is okay, as most butterflies are not active until around 10 a.m. and remain active into the early evening hours.

Make sure butterflies have places to bask in the sunshine. They bask with their wings perpendicular to the sun to gain enough warmth to live. Flowering plants also benefit from sunshine, and those that receive more sunshine will produce more nectar. There are woodland butterflies, but even they venture into the sunlight or bask on occasion.

Situate butterfly gardens in locations protected from your region's prevailing winds. Butterflies gather in places that are a calm respite from the wind. Plant a windbreak of various shrubs and trees to block the wind. Install a fence or vine-covered trellis to break the wind in tight spaces or utilize your home or other buildings as a windbreak. Remember that there will be butterflies from earliest spring into late fall (all year in mild regions), and a sheltered sunny spot will really attract those early-bird or lingering species. This is very important in Indian summer weather, as many butterflies survive frosts in sheltered locations and seek nourishment and warmth on milder days.

Locate butterfly gardens in areas where you can view and enjoy them as well. Butterfly gardens adjacent to outdoor patios and decks and outside family rooms, dining areas or dens are most enjoyable since those are locations where you, your family and guests spend the most time. Your entire yard can become a garden for butterflies as well because there are appropriate plants of all types and sizes that are important for butterflies.

You also can create a variety of habitats (shade, meadow or water gardens, for example) and work to attract many species to your yard—the more variety of places and plants you create, the more species of butterflies you will have (see Garden Design, page 46). Don't dismiss your lawn as an important butterfly habitat—a properly managed lawn will attract many species to your garden (see Lawn Care, page 55).

A sunny yard planted with prairie wildflowers and grasses creates an outstanding site for butterflies.

Site Preparation & Cultural Practices

□ **Soils:** Select plants that are suitable to the soil conditions you have or else you will have to do a lot of work to create favorable conditions. Most gardeners start with a new home where the construction process leaves you with but a few inches of topsoil to grow grass, laid over construction-compacted subsoil—usually concrete-like clay. Besides turf grasses, there are few other plants adapted to such harsh conditions. Many older neighborhoods were constructed at a time when basements were hand dug and usually have better soils. Do some soil tests in areas suitable for your butterfly garden or throughout your property if you're planning a holistic butterfly garden. The best way to break the construction-created hardpan is to amend your soil with organic compost, which breaks up the clay particles and allows air, moisture and nutrients to readily pass through. Support your local community's composting facilities, which make good use of recycled organic refuse. In some difficult situations, you

A do-it-yourself soil test kit.

Recycle kitchen scraps in the compost pile.

may have to build raised beds of good soil.

Start your own compost program now and don't waste an ounce of dead plant material that will quickly become compost. Always place an organic mulch surrounding plants to hold in soil moisture and suppress weeds. In desert areas, stones or pebbles can constitute mulch for drought-tolerant plants.

□ **Horticulture:** All plants also have horticultural requirements that must be met for them to thrive in your butterfly garden and its particular climate. You will have to do some research into any specific growing requirements for each plant recommended.

Plants listed for each region are those most adapted to the climate and soils found in your area, but some may have specific moisture and light requirements. Make use of problematic wet spots or dry spots by incorporating the plants that thrive under such conditions. These problem areas are opportunities to save time, money and resources—especially in water-short regions. Plants also help you create more habitats to attract a wider array of butterflies.

Bright annual marigolds are adapted to most soil conditions across the continent.

Garden Design

The ultimate size and seasonal nature of a plant is the structure by which garden design begins. So are walls, walks, fences—often referred to as hardscape. The "function" of a plant is the building block of the gar-den so you need to learn the characteristics of each plant. Plants are generally grouped into similar hierarchical categories, often called the planting pyramid. Trees—the largest, longest-lived plants—are on top and annual herbs, which are the smallest seasonal (shortest-lived) plants, are on the bottom.

It is wise to invest in trees first because they are there for the long run and take time to establish. Yet you get the most bang for your buck from the annuals. They can create a great display in one season, but most annuals require continued replanting to carry them on from season to season.

The ornamental or aesthetic attributes of a plant are also important in good garden design. The use of ornamental plants and how you combine them really creates beauty in the landscape. A plant's ornamental attributes include beautiful flowers, foliage color, size and shape and how it changes through the seasons, colorful fruit, interesting bark, branching pattern, unique overall shape or silhouette and, most of all, the butterflies that it will attract. You will have to do a little research yourself to see what the recommended butterfly host and nectar plants look like through the seasons.

The functional plant type groups are as follows:

◻ **Shade Trees:** These are the largest deciduous plants that serve as the canopy or overstory trees in the woods. Shade trees lose their leaves in the winter so are seasonally bare branched. They provide cooling shade in summer that is not good for a small butterfly garden but is important in a landscape butterfly garden. Plant shade trees where they will block the sun from your home during the hottest part of the day. You will save immensely on your cooling bills! Shade trees also help hold in warmth in winter and allow winter sunshine through for solar warming of your home.

Paper birch is a large ornamental tree that serves as host plant for numerous northern butterflies.

Evergreens, like this Norway spruce, offer butterflies warm shelter on frosty nights.

Shade tree canopies provide butterflies with frost-free shelter on cold autumn nights until the trees' foliage drops.

❑ **Evergreen Trees:** Evergreen trees are the same size as the shade trees but retain leaves in all seasons. Evergreen trees are important as windbreaks and especially useful between your home and the prevailing winter winds. You can save immensely on your heating bill by proper placement of these trees. Never plant large evergreen trees between your home and the warm winter sun. In snowy regions, avoid planting near driveways and walks, where the trees' shade will prevent snow from melting on sunny winter days. In semitropical regions, large evergreen trees can be used interchangeably with deciduous shade trees, yet even in south Florida the winter sun can be welcome.

Evergreen trees are important in mild-winter climates in providing warmer microclimates under their canopies on frosty winter nights where butterflies can find shelter and protection from the cold.

❑ **Small Trees:** Small trees offer what we designers call "human scale" to a landscape. They are trees between 15 and 30 feet and never mature at heights over 50 feet. They are usually free of branches above our head height and not much taller than our homes. They create a comfortable, room-like space beneath and between them and do not cast as much shade as shade trees. Utilize them like shade trees where you have less space.

Deciduous small trees lose their leaves in winter or drought periods and allow sunshine to stream through. Many small deciduous trees are among the most beautiful of flowering plants, while others produce beautiful fruit or

have exquisite bark and branching characteristics.

Small evergreen trees have the same function in the landscape as small deciduous trees but, because they hold their foliage in winter, make better winter screens from both wind and unsightly views. Small evergreen trees also block welcome winter sun so should be used appropriately. Small evergreen trees may have great ornamental bloom or fruit but most are grown for their unique foliage at all seasons.

❑ **Shrubs:** Shrubs are multi-stemmed woody plants that reach anywhere from knee-high to 10 feet tall. They can be further classified by their size and by whether they are

Small trees, like this crabapple, offer butterflies flowers for nectaring, as well as twigs and branches for resting spots.

deciduous or evergreen. Many shrubs are excellent host plants and some even have nectar-rich blooms that attract butterflies.

Evergreen shrubs retain their foliage year-round so are

Weigelia, a great flowering shrub for butterflies.

ful bloom and fruit production to hand-some foliage and interesting bark and branching patterns.

Small shrubs are the woody plants that usually reach knee-high to shoulder height at maturity. Most adults can easily see over these plants, and their foliage-holding characteristic of being deciduous or evergreen has less functional value and more of an ornamental value because of the size of the plants. They are great for winter interest and their small size. Many produce beautiful flowers and foliage but do not die to the ground each winter as a perennial would.

▫ **Vines:** Vines may be deciduous or ever-green woody plants, as well as herbaceous perennials or annuals. Vines are plants that take on the shape or form of the objects on which they climb. They have no internal structure of their own so they

quite important in enlivening the winter landscape. They work best to create screens to views you wish blocked all year. They can block low winds and create small, sheltered spaces ideal for butterfly gardens. Because of their smaller size, their winter shadows are less of a problem in blocking winter sun. They still can create shaded patches on walks and driveways where winter ice and snow would otherwise melt.

Large deciduous shrubs are the woody plants that reach head height and higher at maturity, and can be used as visual screens because we cannot see over them. They lose their leaves in winter and open up views and sun spaces in that season. Their ornamental attributes vary from beauti-

Butterflies love to nectar on passionflower.

Bottlebrush buckeye is a good shrub for a butterfly yard and garden.

utilize companion plants, walls, fences or buildings for sup-port. They are valuable because of their 2-dimensional quality and suitability for use in tight spaces. Several species are prime butterfly host plants and a few are great nectar sources too.

▫ **Perennials:** Perennials are herbaceous plants that live through multiple growing seasons. Their above-ground portions die back in winter and new growth emerges in spring. Perennials usually have superior ornamental blooming and foliage attributes that make them a beautiful addition to borders of yards and outdoor spaces. They have

Milkweed, the Monarch's host plant.

A Cabbage White nectars on the blossoms of Russian sage.

the wonderful value of not having to be replaced each year. Many are nectar rich and serve as butterfly host plants.

▫ **Biennials:** Biennials are plants that live 2 years. The first year they grow foliage, usually basal and ground hugging. The second year they bloom, set seed and die. Most biennials set copious amounts of seed and self-sow to perpetuate themselves in the garden.

▫ **Annuals:** Annuals are plants that live just one growing season—they flower, fruit and die in that time period. Some tropical perennials, shrubs and even trees can be treated as annuals in most of the country.

Annuals have the longest bloom season and most are superior sources of nectar for butterflies. They do require continued replanting each year to perpetuate themselves. Some annuals self-sow—in other words, reseed themselves—and come back on their own from year to year. Annuals make great subjects for containers and planters for spring, summer, fall and, in the mild South and far West, winter as well.

A Monarch nectars on a zinnia.

Nectar Plants

Flowering plants produce blossoms rich in nectar (sugar water) to attract various pollinators. Those plants that utilize butterflies to pollinate their flowers are the nectaring plants listed in this book.

Most adult butterflies eat sugar for energy to live and actively seek nectar-rich flowers to feed on. Butterflies eat using their proboscis, which is composed of two long tongues rolled up together under the butterfly's head. They unroll the proboscis into their food and it functions as a straw for them to suck their liquid nourishment.

Each butterfly species chooses particular plants from which to nectar. Those with long proboscises can nectar from long tubular flowers while others can only nectar from flowers with nectar available near the surface. Some butterflies seek certain colors to guide them to nectar-rich flowers. The shape of the blossom or group of flowers is also important as a landing pad for butterflies of a particular species.

Select and cultivate flowering plants that are recommended to attract butterflies in your region. Butterflies are very regional in some of their nectar choices but those plants listed in the following chapters are some of the most tried-and-true. Watch butterflies' choices through the seasons and add or subtract nectaring plants accordingly.

Butterfly bush, *Verbena bonariensis* and Mexican sunflowers are universally the best three nectar plants nationwide, and are a sure bet to immediately attract butterflies into your garden.

Butterfly bush languishes in the Southwest and semitropics. It is a large shrub in the South and Pacific West, a perennial in the Midwest and Northeast and an annual in

Butterfly bushes of any hue make outstanding nectar plants.

coldest winter portions of the Northern Great Plains and Canadian Zone!

A butterfly garden with more than the top few species of butterfly nectaring plants will attract even more species of butterflies in the long run. It is also more environmentally sound because the greater the diversity of plants you grow, the less chance that diseases and pests will run amok.

Integrate nectaring plants from a variety of heights and plant types too. Some butterflies are denizens of the forest canopy and will seldom fly down to nectar on ground-hugging plants, while others prefer to stay near the ground and nectar mainly on low plants.

Always observe how butterflies utilize a plant before you install it in your butterfly garden. First visit your local botanical garden, natural area or nursery and watch whether butterflies are utilizing a particular flower (you can also check the North American Butterfly Association's website at www.naba.org).

Many new hybrid plants are rich in nectar but many are not. Many double-flowering varieties of plants also may have no nectar or no way for butterflies to reach it. Most hybrid roses fall into this category but some otherwise great butterfly flowers do too—for instance, fully double-flowering types of zinnias provide nowhere for butterflies to nectar.

Verbena is one of the top three nectar choices for butterflies across the continent.

Host Plants

H ost plants are those that the caterpillars of a particular species of butterfly eat. There is no plant that feeds all sorts of caterpillars. Most plants only host one or a few related species.

When you select which host plants to include in your garden, start with those plants that feed the butterflies you already have in your garden. Next, identify your favorite butterflies in your region and habitat that require a specific host plant to be present. Plant those unique host plant species and in the long run you are apt to attract some of its host-specific butterflies. Be patient, because it may take more than one season for the butterflies to find and colonize your garden.

Some of the easiest nationwide butterflies to begin with include the Monarch, which is a migrant butterfly that can be attracted in each region by planting any milkweed

Bronze fennel is sure to host Black or Anise Swallowtails in your yard or garden.

species. The tropical milkweed, bloodflower, is a naturalized perennial in Florida and does well as a garden perennial in mild zones and as an annual everywhere else. Plant a few of the local native species particular to your region as well.

The Painted Lady is a colonist butterfly for all of the continent. Its caterpillars feed on plants in the thistle and mallow families—so planting those appropriate for your region will virtually guarantee Painted Ladies in your garden all summer. Otherwise they will just pass through and nectar.

The Black and Anise Swallowtails are beautiful butterflies that together are resident butterflies from coast to coast. They share some of the same host plants that survive in every garden region as well—plants in the carrot family, namely fennel, dill and parsley, which are grown in perennial, herb and vegetable gardens.

Except for the ubiquitous few mentioned above, make sure to plant the host plants appropriate in your garden region. You will not attract butterflies that are not found in your region, and some species do vary their host plant from region to region.

Many host plants do not conform to the tidiness or aesthetic attributes required of most landscape plants. Many of the "lady" butterflies' caterpillars feed only on plants in the nettle family, including the hurtful stinging nettle. Can you find a place to have a stand of this otherwise nuisance plant? Find an out-of-the-way nook screened by a grouping of shrubs, a trellis or shed to provide a place for such weeds.

Lawn grasses and lawn weeds also host a plethora of butterfly caterpillars, so be sure to review the lawn care section (page 55) to ensure proper management of your lawn to encourage butterflies.

Many species of mallow including this marsh mallow (the original source of marshmallows) make excellent host plants for several species of butterflies.

Non-Floral Butterfly Attractors

Some butterflies do not get nourishment from nectar and prefer other sources for sugary nourishment. Some butterflies like sweet tree sap—often utilizing the handiwork of any of our sapsucker woodpeckers to provide a place to drink sap. A lot of butterflies also like the sweets of overripe fruit. Fruit trees make excellent additions

The Hoary Comma, like many butterflies, is cryptically colored and patterned to blend in with its surroundings.

to butterfly gardens for this reason, and many fruit trees have nectar-rich spring blossoms that attract early butterflies as well. Apples, cherries, peaches and plums attract butterflies with both nectar-rich flowers and aromatic overripe fruit. The fruit of persimmons and figs often ferments with age and attracts a myriad of butterflies.

Many male butterflies—especially swallowtails, sulphurs and blues—need extra minerals and salts gained from mud. These butterflies are actually not drinking the water when they gather at puddles or wet shorelines; they are removing trace elements from the water. Groups of various male butterflies gathered in such locations are called puddle parties. This is what is referred to if a butterfly "puddles." Many butterflies (both male and female) of arid regions do need to drink water to survive and are actually imbibing the moisture for their survival.

You can also make a butterfly feeder to attract those butterflies that like overripe fruit, especially if you don't have the space for a fruit tree. Here's how.

Place overripe fruit into a hanging basket with a water reservoir to collect excess rainfall. Be sure to hang feeders out of reach of critters like raccoons and oppossums. The basket sides help hide the ugly fruit but hide the butterflies

too unless you peer in for a closer look. Any style of hanging birdbath also works but will hold water in rainy weather.

A couple of times a week, add more grapes, bananas and rinds of mango, canteloupe, watermelon or whatever fruit you have left over. You can see the butterflies swirling around the feeder, often alighting on the side and creeping into the stash.

Place your butterfly feeder where you can view it from your patio or deck. Butterfly feeders may also bait flies and wasps away from outdoor activities.

Butterfly feeders will increase the kinds of butterflies you attract to your garden. Butterflies that will attend them include: California Sister, Commas, Emperors, Lorquin's Admiral, Morning Cloak, Pearly-Eyes, Question Mark, Red Admiral, Red-Spotted Purple, Viceroy, Weidemeyer's Admiral, White Admiral and Wood-Nymphs.

Apple trees offer nectar-rich blossoms, leaves which host several species' caterpillars, and fallen fruit for many types of butterflies to feed on—a perfect small tree for the butterfly garden.

Habitat Considerations

Many species of butterflies need untidy nooks created by brushpiles, woodpiles, dead or decaying trees or limbs, even uncompacted leaf piles, for places to hibernate through the winter. It is also important to leave a lot of the dead stalks of your perennials standing through the winter. These stems often harbor overwintering caterpillars or chrysalises! The stalks will provide winter interest for you, and many of them, such as purple coneflowers, contain seeds that attract birds, which enliven the yard during the butterflies' off-season.

Don't always prune all the dead branches out of the old trees in your back lot if they do not pose a threat to utilities, yourself or neighbors, or affect the health of other trees. Place all pruned and fallen twigs, branches and other woody "refuse" in a pile near the compost. Don't disturb the pile all through the winter. Chip, cut or break it up into mulch after spring has arrived and the overwintering butterflies have left. Note that a butterfly house is seldom utilized by butterflies and is really most effective as garden decor.

Some of the best nectar-producing flowering plants are not gardenworthy and are too weedy for the flower border. Allow a corner of your property to go wild and have some of those untidy weeds that many butterflies use as host and nectar plants.

In small lots, let various wild grasses and sedges, clovers, frost aster, daisy fleabane and lamb's quarters grow behind ornamental perennials and shrubs against a back fence. Many of these weedy plants are cool-season, winter-blooming plants in the South, spring-blooming plants in most of the country and summer-blooming plants in the far North and at high elevations. They provide nectar at a season when most garden plants have not yet kicked into bloom.

In larger lots and acreages, newly accepted styles of landscaping incorporate a natural look into the scheme. Why do many of us mow an acre-size lot when we utilize so little of this lawn space? Reduce your lawn and plant a meadow or prairie or just maintain the weedy wildflowers that self-sow into a former lawn. These spaces will vastly increase the numbers and varieties of butterflies you attract to your garden anywhere in the nation.

The most important facts to deal with in a natural garden are: 1) inform your neighbors of what you are doing and why; 2) maintain a clean edge to the wild area; 3) provide a lawn buffer between wild landscapes and your home in case of fire, especially important in fire-prone regions such as the West and South; 4) sign your natural landscape so that others learn that it has an intended purpose. Many native landscaping organizations like "Wild Ones" provide such signage. You will save a lot of time and gasoline, create less noise and air pollution and just have a more enjoyable life to spend with your newfound butterfly compadres.

If you move to a new home, take some time to explore your new neighborhood and see how your garden fits in with its natural surroundings and butterfly habitat. This is finding your "context."

Are you in a sea of new housing where everyone has a few trees and a lawn? Or are you in an old neighborhood with mature plantings? Do you have an agricultural area nearby? Are you close or adjacent to a stream or river with natural habitat along its banks? A natural park or preserve? Woodland or grassland (old field, meadow or prairie) nearby?

Your garden's context is important, as the adjacent habitat dictates what butterflies you can expect to have in your garden. Some butterflies are wide ranging and show up anywhere, while others may do the same but stay close to certain habitat types and corridors.

My house sits adjacent to an old hedgerow of trees that link me to the surrounding countryside. Many butterflies (and other wildlife) follow this "greenspace" corridor into my suburban context and discover my butterfly oasis. Greenspace corridors vastly increase the number of species of butterflies and wildlife in your neighborhood.

A meadow filled with wild bergamot provides outstanding habitat for butterflies.

Pesticide Use and Misuse

"Probably no other animal is more symbolic of a clean, healthy environment than the butterfly. Butterflies are ideal monitors for habitat destruction, pollution and applications of chemicals such as pesticides and herbicides. For this reason, the symbol of the butterfly is frequently employed to epitomize everything that is good, clean and healthy."—Dr. Gary Noel Ross.

The biggest mistake with pesticide application is our ignorance. Homeowners are the biggest consumer of pesticides—more than all farmers, ranchers and professional landscape managers (i.e. golf courses) combined! While the professionals must take an exam to get licensed in pesticide use, anyone can go down to the local hardware or discount store and purchase pesticides. Please read labels carefully and comply with what is stated.

Pesticides kill butterflies and they kill them in all stages—eggs, caterpillars, chrysalises, adult butterflies. Inorganic pesticides that leave residues even kill the butterflies that visit later.

A good approach to a healthy, butterfly-friendly yard and garden is as follows: Practice Plant Health Care (PHC). We have all learned to eat right and exercise to take care of ourselves. In gardening we can do the same for our plants. If you plant hardy plants adapted to your climate, rainfall, soil and water, and fertilize only as needed, you will have a more healthy and vigorous plant that is more resistant to pest and disease attacks. Overwatered and overfertilized plants are our biggest mistakes.

You should also practice Integrated Pest Management (IPM), which means controlling pests only when you have

Lacewings are good bugs that, along with butterflies, can be killed by overzealous use of pesticides.

a significant problem, and then target just that pest and don't spray beyond its presence. If you have just a few aphids, the ladybugs and lacewings will take care of them for you. If you have a major problem on a specific plant, then target only that specific plant and use the least detrimental control. If you blanket spray, remember, you kill the good bugs (butterflies, bees, ladybugs, lacewings, etc.) too!

Use an organic pesticide that kills just what it comes in contact with when you use it and does not leave a residue that kills future butterflies. Safers soap, pyrethrins and rotenone are examples of organic pesticides. Don't be fooled that these chemicals are safe, as they are very toxic and must be handled properly (as per their respective labels) just like their inorganic counterparts.

I gave up chemicals in my wildlife-friendly garden altogether and enjoy more than 60 species of butterflies in my garden. A massive outbreak of aphids on black-eyed Susans growing among partridge peas taught me a big lesson. No way was I going to spray these plants and endanger the flock of nectaring Pearl Crescents on the black-eyed Susans or harm the caterpillars of Cloudless, Sleepy and Little Sulphurs present on the partridge peas. The ladybugs and lacewings finally came to my rescue and kept the aphid population to below damaging levels. I resisted temptation to spray and the patience paid off with a healthy yard full of beautiful butterflies.

Ladybugs are beneficial insects that feast on pesky aphids.

Lawn Care
Compatible with Butterflies

How do you identify a beautiful lawn? Is it one with uniform dense green grass and not a weed in sight? If so, you have described a lawn that is *not* compatible with butterflies. A butterfly lawn is one that is lush green and varied and has only things in it that don't prick your feet when you walk barefoot across it. White clover, frogfruit and even the occasional plantain and dandelion are celebrated. It's perfectly okay to have such a lawn!

The number-one detriment to butterflies and the biggest mistake in proper lawn care is that people mow their lawns too short. By mowing your lawn year-round on the highest (rather than lowest) setting, you provide more space for those butterfly caterpillars that are invisibly feeding on the lawn grasses. In summer when the heat and dryness threaten your grass, the longer length provides a shadier, cooler root zone and the neighbors' scalped grass needs more water to prevent it from burning out. Simply, mow high year-round.

Another component of a healthy lawn that has gone out of vogue, yet at one time was a mainstay of a healthy lawn, is white clover. Plant it if you don't have it! White clover is a legume that inoculates nitrogen into the soil and thus into the grass so you won't have to fertilize. It blooms in the winter in the South, in spring and fall in much of the country and all summer in cool summer regions. White clover blooms are rich in nectar for butterflies, and its flowers and foliage serve as a host plant to many species of butterflies as well. You will also help the local bee population with the nectar-rich blooms. Our forefathers who included white clover in every standard lawn mix were wise indeed.

Natural landscapes need proper management as well to promote butterflies. Woodlands, meadows and wetlands are all threatened by exotic vegetation that chokes out many native plants that butterflies need as hosts or for nectar. Gardeners are familiar with invasive plants like buckthorns, Japanese honeysuckle, Chinese privet, kudzu, loosestrife, melaleuca, tamarisk and lythrum that invade and overtake natural landscapes. Remove invasive exotic plants and keep an eye out for them. Fire is also a tool in managing these landscapes—just remember, it kills butterflies in all stages. Never burn an entire landscape, and be sure to leave some known butterfly host plants unburned.

Old-time lawns contained a lot of clover. It's attractive, not a weed, and it will draw butterflies. Consider adding a little clover to your yard.

Butterfly Gardening Tips

Butterflies in the Food Chain

Butterflies have a difficult life. They go through a lot of trouble to exist at all, and have ongoing obstacles throughout their entire metamorphosis.

Microbes we can't even see are butterflies' biggest enemy; we utilize one of them, the bacteria *Bacillus thuren-*gensis (Bt) in the pesticide against caterpillars. Other predatory insects, like trichogramma wasps and praying mantis, also prey upon butterflies and are offered as biological controls in many gardening catalogs. Ambush bugs, crab spiders, wheel bugs, various wasps, flies and many others feed on butterflies on a daily basis. Quite a few wasps and flies parasitize caterpillars in grotesque fashion by living and growing inside them.

Many birds eat butterflies in the caterpillar, chrysalis and adult stage—my flock of Cloudless Sulphurs was reduced one fall day when a migrating Eastern Wood Pewee (a type of flycatcher) made it rain yellow butterfly wings. But all these natural predators keep butterfly populations in balance. Butterflies lay hundreds of eggs. Unlike a bird, which may lay only a few eggs and nest once or twice a year, a butterfly has many more chances to replace itself. Sometimes butterflies are very successful and there are population explosions of certain species. Little Sulphurs, American Snouts, Painted Ladies, Califor-

A crab spider holds a Red Admiral in a deadly embrace.

A wheelbug drinks from a newly formed Monarch chrysalis.

A tiny ant-like parasitic wasp emerged from this doomed Black Swallowtail chrysalis.

where hundreds of thousands of butterflies emerge. Many get slaughtered by cars along roadsides during such events.

Another big enemy to butterflies is the bulldozer, destroying habitat. A silent problem is the excess deer herd that has denuded the understory of many woodlands and destroyed butterfly host plants, thus upsetting the balance of predators and leaving butterflies even more vulnerable to attack. Support local efforts to keep deer populations in balance.

We can help butterflies by following the gardening suggestions in this book. Most butterflies will readily venture into our specially designed and planted butterfly gardens, and prosper. Gardeners have already saved the Atala butterfly in Florida and now it flourishes. There are still species that don't benefit by our butterfly gardens.

Many butterflies are habitat restricted and won't venture into our human-created landscapes. This is good reason to protect remnants of natural forest, grassland and wetlands found in your community. Though this book deals with the butterflies you can help, it does have a few footnotes, namely about the larger fritillaries, which need habitat protection and proper management assistance beyond our gardens.

nia Tortoiseshells, Red Admirals and Hackberry Emperors are just a few species that seem to have periodic explosions

A Great Spangled Fritillary caught in a spider's web.

A Clouded Sulphur on the grill of an automobile.

Butterfly Gardening Tips

SWALLOWTAILS

*S*wallowtails are the largest and most flamboyant of butterflies. Their size and beauty make them among the most recognizable and cherished butterflies in the garden. Swallowtails get their name from the tails on their hind wings and at least two species can be found in almost every garden in North America. Their caterpillars have a most unique defense mechanism—when disturbed, they exude from behind their heads two fleshy, foul-scented horns, called osmeterium. The nasty scent deters would-be predators. The typical swallowtail chrysalis does not hang upside down, like most butterflies'. Rather, it is suspended by a silken thread around its middle.

Pipevine Swallowtail

Battus philenor

The Pipevine Swallowtail was not named for its looks—as with three other swallowtails, it was named for its host plant. An old common name—"Blue Swallowtail"—readily describes its most dramatic feature: the unique, hard-to-describe iridescent blue-green reflection on its

A Pipevine Swallowtail nectars on a hybrid bergamot blossom.

hind wings, which have a metallic, oily appearance unlike any other American butterfly.

The pipevine name is, however, this butterfly's most distinguishing characteristic, as it gains its unique attributes from this plant. The toxic compounds found in the pipevine plant are utilized by this butterfly to make it unpalatable to birds and mammals that try to eat it. A bird who gets sick on a Pipevine Swallowtail caterpillar or butterfly learns not to eat another one like it. Many other butterfly species mimic it to avoid predation. Some female Eastern Tiger Swallowtails, all female Black Swallowtails, female Spicebush Swallowtails, Red-Spotted Purples and female Dianas have this same black-and-blue pattern to fool birds into thinking they're a bad-tasting Pipevine Swallowtail.

A hardy resident butterfly, the Pipevine Swallowtail survives the winter as a chrysalis.

◻ **Habitat:** Pipevine Swallowtails reside in forests, woodlands, savannas and urban areas where pipevine grows wild or for ornament. They readily venture into open country such as grasslands and desert in search of nectar.

◻ **Garden Habit:** Pipevine Swallowtails flutter continually while nectaring. They rest only to bask in sunshine. Males are territorial and perch in a favorite location, which they return to after chasing intruding males and courting potential mates.

◻ **Garden Nectar Plants:** shrub: late-blooming garden lilacs; perennials: anise hyssop, columbines, paintbrush, Jupiter's beard, blazingstars, wild bergamot, lyre-leaf sage, blue dicks, rose verbena; biennials: Indian paintbrushes, native thistles, dame's rocket; annuals: lantana, pentas, tropical sage, coral porterweed, Mexican sunflower, *Verbena bonariensis*, zinnias. Pipevine Swallowtails have a long proboscis and can nectar at longer-tubed flowers than most swallowtails.

◻ **Garden Host Plants:** vines: California pipevine, Dutchman's pipe (the most common pipevine at garden centers) and woolly pipevine, which is available only at nurseries that specialize in native plants; perennial: Virginia snakeroot.

Pipevine Swallowtail temporarily expanded its range northward in Victorian times with the fashion of planting Dutchman's pipe on porches, verandas and pergolas. It has again expanded northward with a resurgence of this vine's popularity and increased awareness of gardening for butterflies.

◻ **Identification:** 2.5 to 5 inches. The only "black" swallowtail with blue-green iridescence, white spots and *no* yellow or orange on their upper side. Males' iridescent blue-green wash is showy and dramatic, while females appear flat black with only a hint of iridescence on the hind wings. There are no fake eye spots near the swallowtails.

◻ **Caterpillar:** Pipevine Swallowtail caterpillars are a dramatic black with jester-like red tubercles. This pattern displays typical warning coloration to predators. They feed in a

The unique flower of the pipevine—host to and namesake of the Pipevine Swallowtail.

TIPS

TO ATTRACT

Plant a pipevine of any of the three listed species. Females are always on the lookout for plants to lay their eggs on. Any late-blooming lilac is a sure bet to lure in thirsty spring brood butterflies to colonize your garden. Plant a flower border of tall, airy coral porterweed and blue-violet *Verbena bonariensis* blooming above a mass of lantana. Native gardeners should plant a stand of long-blooming anise hyssop.

herd on the underside of a leaf when young and act fearless when older, as they are distasteful to birds. They display bright yellow osmeteria when they are disturbed.

▫ **Chrysalis:** Pipevine Swallowtail's chrysalis is distinctly S-shaped, with a golden saddle, protruding bumps and ridges and of cryptic pink, green or brown coloration.

▫ **Local Relative:** The Polydamas Swallowtail, Tailless or Gold Rim Swallowtail (*Battus polydamas*), is a tropical swallowtail commonly found in gardens of south Florida and Texas.

A Pipevine Swallowtail displays its dusky colors.

Zebra Swallowtail

Eurytides marcellus

The aptly named Zebra Swallowtail may be colored like its well-known namesake for exactly the same reason! Just as the striped zebra on the Serengeti appears unclear to the lion, this swallowtail appears a difficult target for a hungry bird. The butterfly enhances this

A Zebra Swallowtail nectars on a butterfly milkweed.

broken-pattern image by continually fluttering. Their rocket-like hurried flight makes them appear a blur to the gardener as well. Zebra Swallowtails are closely tied to their host plant, so much so that it probably could be called the pawpaw swallowtail. They are rarely found far from pawpaws, and their native range follows that of the pawpaw and its deep South cousins to a tee. It is our only swallowtail from a tropical group known

as "kite" swallowtails, aptly named for their aerodynamic wings and long streamer tails. Kite swallowtails' host plants are in the tropical custard apple family, of which only one species, the pawpaw, is found in temperate regions. The Zebra Swallowtail has the longest swallowtails of any in our region and the summer broods' tails are even 50 percent longer than their spring parents'. Zebra Swallowtails are among the first butterflies to emerge in spring, after which male Zebra Swallowtails often form puddle parties along rivers and streams. Summer broods are less common and rarely puddle.

▫ **Status:** A hardy resident butterfly, Zebra Swallowtail survives the winter as a chrysalis. They occasionally stray northward.

▫ **Habitat:** Zebra Swallowtails reside in woodlands near pawpaw, which often grows in floodplain forests and along wooded streams and ravines. In the deep South, they also inhabit pine savannas, flatwoods and scrub where species of shrubby pawpaws grow wild.

▫ **Garden Habit:** This swallowtail is infrequent in gardens, but readily attracted if you are near habitat where pawpaws grow wild. They usually just zip by, but females can't resist pawpaw and will pause to lay eggs and then investigate the whole garden. They also lay over to nectar and can become quite docile and approachable while nectaring on their favorite flowers.

▫ **Garden Nectar Plants:** shrubs: butterfly bush, blackberries, blueberries; perennials: dogbanes, spring beauty, milkweeds—especially butterflyweed, rose verbena; annuals: Spanish needles, zinnias.

▫ **Garden Host Plants:** small tree: pawpaw; shrubs: flag pawpaws, long-leaf pawpaw, small-flowered pawpaw, dwarf pawpaw, flatwoods pawpaw and squirrel-bananas.

▫ **Identification:** 2.5 to 4 inches. The zebra pattern is unmistakable, and it is the only black-and-white swallowtail in the East. The undersides of the wings have an exquisite turquoise tint with a red band midway across the hind wing.

Pawpaw flowers—a great host plant for the Zebra Swallowtail.

Plant a pawpaw tree in mid-Atlantic, upper South and lower Midwest regions, or any of the pawpaw shrubs in the deep South. Females are continually searching for these plants to lay eggs on and will "taste" all comparable-looking plants, such as magnolias. Zebra Swallowtails' all-time favorite source of nectar is the butterflyweed, so planting several will ensure that you attract hungry butterflies. They will readily colonize your garden if pawpaws are planted.

The fake eye spots by the swallowtails are red.

□ **Caterpillar:** Zebra Swallowtail caterpillars are a shy sage green with bluish, black and yellow "shoulder" bands. Some mature caterpillars may be yellow or black striped. They display yellow osmeteria when disturbed. An army of creatures, from other insects to birds, readily prey upon the caterpillars; the result is that it has the lowest survival rate of any swallowtail's caterpillars in my garden.

□ **Chrysalis:** Zebra Swallowtail's chrysalis is hump-backed with a squared-off look—compact and smaller than any other swallowtail chrysalis. Its coloration is cryptic green (summer only) or brown.

A Zebra Swallowtail basking. This is the only black-and-white swallowtail in the East.

Black Swallowtail

Papilio polyxenes

The Black Swallowtail's old name, "Common Eastern Swallowtail," might be more appropriate because it is one of the most common swallowtails in the eastern two-thirds of temperate America.

It is one of the easiest swallowtails to attract to gardens throughout its range, and one of the easiest to raise and watch metamorphose from egg to adult. The Black Swallowtail has adapted well to the agricultural and suburban landscape we have created across much of the United States and lower Canada. In the western portions of our region there are several swallowtails that look like the Black Swallowtail but most of the look-alikes haven't adapted to our gardens and are displaced by suburban development. The male and female Black Swallowtail look so different that they appear to be different species of butterflies. The female mimics the distasteful Pipevine Swallowtail to convince would-be predators that it is equally distasteful, when in fact it would be a tasty morsel.

□ **Status:** A hardy resident butterfly, Black Swallowtail survives the winter as a chrysalis.

□ **Habitat:** Black Swallowtails reside in open deserts, marshes, meadows and prairies as well as vacant lots and gardens in urban areas. They may be common in gardens and readily attracted and reared.

□ **Garden Habit:** Black Swallowtails are usually fluttery while they nectar but are occasionally docile as they nectar on their favorite flowers. Females search the lawn and gar-

den for appropriate host plants to lay eggs on. Males seldom visit the garden except to nectar unless an extensive flower border or meadow is present where they may take up territory and peruse the same space over and over, chasing off rival males and courting visiting females.

A Black Swallowtail caterpillar.

□ **Garden Nectar Plants:** perennials: milkweeds, Joe-Pye-weed, blazingstars, rosinweed, clovers, Rose verbena; biennial: native thistles; annuals: bloodflower, lantana, pentas, marigolds, tithonia, *Verbena bonariensis*, zinnias.

□ **Garden Host Plants:** perennials: bronze fennel, alexanders, occasionally garden rue, turpentine broom; biennials: parsley, fennel, carrots/Queen-Anne's lace, common parsnip (the wild form is poisonous to the touch on sunny days!); annuals: dill, celery, lovage, anise.

□ **Identification:** 3 to 4.5 inches. A medium-sized black-colored swallowtail that is sexually dimorphic (males look different from females). Males have two beautiful and distinctive bands of yellow spots. The inner band on the hind wing is pronounced. Females are blacker overall with extensive blue on the hind wing. She mimics the Pipevine Swallowtail and can readily be confused with other Pipevine Swallowtail mimics. Female Spicebush Swallowtails are most similar in the East, "Baird's" Old World Swallowtail and dark forms of Anise Swallowtails in the West. (See Anise Swallowtail for details.)

□ **Caterpillar:** Early stages of the Black Swallowtail caterpillar look like a small bird dropping to avoid predation. Older caterpillars are green with black stripes and yellow spotting. The caterpillars

Naturalize your yard with white clover to help attract Black Swallowtails.

The Gardener's Butterfly Book

can be extremely variable—often predominantly black at the end of the growing season. The caterpillars are readily in view on garden host plants but are left alone by most birds though they often fall prey to wasps and flies.

□ **Chrysalis:** Black Swallowtails pupate on nearby plants, shrubs or structures and can be cryptic, striated green, brown or gray to match their location. Their overall appearance is that of a broken twig stub with sharp pointed projections on their head.

A male Black Swallowtail nectaring on lantana.

Anise Swallowtail

Papilio zalacaon

The Anise Swallowtail is the western counterpart to the Black Swallowtail, and its caterpillars, chrysalises and some of the butterflies themselves cannot be differentiated. The Anise Swallowtail is basically a more colorfully yellow male-looking Black Swallowtail and, unlike the sexually dimorphic Black Swallowtail, male and female Anise Swallowtails look the same. If you live in California,

An Old World Swallowtail basking—this is a close relative of the Anise Swallowtail.

the Pacific Northwest or Rocky Mountains, then this is the swallowtail you will most likely have in your garden.

This butterfly's old name—"Western Swallowtail"—describes its place in North America, and its current name—Anise Swallowtail—describes how it has adapted to our changed modern world. This butterfly almost never dines on its wild host plants as its tastes have changed to a more Old World menu. With the settlement of California by the Spanish, anise (actually more aptly called sweet fennel), was brought here for culinary purposes and to be placed on the floors of missions so that it would exude a pleasant scent when walked upon. Native to the Mediterranean, this plant escaped and now thrives as a wildflower. The Anise Swallowtail soon found this plant to its liking and has prospered on it ever since. Just like the Black Swallowtail in the East, this butterfly is one of the easiest to

attract and raise in your garden.

❏ **Status:** A hardy resident butterfly, Anise Swallowtail survives the winter as a chrysalis.

❏ **Habitat:** Anise Swallowtails reside in open country like mountain meadows, prairies, old fields and suburbs. It cannot survive in forests or deserts. In urban environments, they thrive in vacant lots and roadsides as well as in gardens with their host plants. This butterfly frequents hilltops to search for a mate—a practice known as "hill-topping" in butterfly lingo—"cruising for chicks/guys" in ours.

❏ **Garden Habit:** Anise Swallowtail is common in gardens and is the western counterpart to Black Swallowtail. This butterfly presides in gardens all year in southern California.

❏ **Garden Nectar Plants:** shrubs: butterfly bush, lantanas, cape plumbago, rosemary, purple sage, garden lilacs; perennials: columbines, Jupiter's beard, wild buckwheats, blue sage, rose verbena; biennials: native thistles, sweet William; annuals: impatiens, lantanas.

❏ **Garden Host Plants:** small tree: citrus; perennial: sanicles; biennials: angelica, fennel, carrots/ Queen-Anne's lace, parsley; annual: dill.

❏ **Caterpillar:** Anise Swallowtail's caterpillar is nearly identical to that of the Black Swallowtail.

❏ **Chrysalis:** Anise Swallowtail's chrysalis is the same as that of the Black Swallowtail.

❏ **Identification:** 2.75 to 3.5 inches. Typical forms you are most likely to encounter in your garden have distinctive extensive yellow coloration in the form of broad yellow bands or patches with black wing veins. Other forms of this butterfly are similar to Black Swallowtail but this butterfly's abdomen has yellow bands or dashes, not spots, down its sides. There is a centered black pupil in its fake swallowtail eye spots. You may encounter many localized varieties in the West but they are usually limited in occurrence and absent from gardens. Anise Swallowtail may hybridize with Black Swallowtail where their ranges meet.

❏ **Local Relative:** Old World Swallowtail (*Papilio machaon*). Old World Swallowtail is a common swallowtail of the

TIPS
TO ATTRACT

Plant dill in your vegetable or herb garden, curly parsley edging in your annual flower bed and bronze fennel in your perennial garden to attract Anise Swallowtails to your garden. This butterfly has changed its favored food plant to these imported plants but will occasionally use its native carrot family host plants.

western wildlands, including Alaska. Host plants are artemisias and it has two prevalent subspecies, including: Oregon Swallowtail (*P. machaon* ssp. *oregonius*), the official state butterfly of Oregon, and Baird's Swallowtail or Western Black Swallowtail (*Papilio machaon* ssp. *bairdii*). Recent DNA fingerprinting has enabled us to learn that these swallowtails are all one species despite looking quite different from one another. They do have the same habits and food plants. Their most consistent identification field mark is that these swallowtails' fake eye spots' pupils are absent or, if present, dash shaped or not centered.

An Anise Swallowtail, the most common garden swallowtail in the West.

Giant Swallowtail

Papilio cresphontes

The Latin name describes this swallowtail well, as Crestephonte was one of the Herculids who claimed to be a descendant of Hercules of Greek mythology. Giant Swallowtail is the disputed largest butterfly in North America; the Two-Tailed Swallowtail in the Rocky Mountains and some Eastern Tiger Swallowtails in Florida are

A Giant Swallowtail nectars with wings outspread on a zinnia.

giant too. Female, summer-brood Giant Swallowtails often attain wingspans slightly over 6 inches.

Giant Swallowtails were once a tropical species but, for some reason, in the 1890s they began appearing in places like western Pennsylvania. They have now colonized and become residents over all of the South, most of the hot-summer Southwest (as recently as 1960s) and the South and central Midwest, where its new host plant, prickly-ashes, are prevalent. Some summers, Giant Swallowtails are the most common swallowtail in the upper Midwest near the Mississippi River. Most references incorrectly treat this butterfly as a stray or colonist outside of the South.

▫ **Status:** A hardy resident butterfly, the Giant Swallowtail survives the winter as a chrysalis. It is a colonist or irregular stray summer visitor to the northernmost portion of its range.

▫ **Habitat:** Giant Swallowtails are creatures of forests, woodlands, savannas and treed urban areas. They will venture into adjacent grasslands and deserts in search of nec-

tar. They are common in gardens and seem to love all the neotropical annual flowers that we have imported from their presettlement homelands.

▫ **Garden Habit:** Giant Swallowtails flutter continually while nectaring, their upper wings touching at their lower base while their hind wings are held outspread. They appear a very confusing blur to a predator, and the brown spot in the yellow "X" of their forewing gives them a menacing facial look. This butterfly is readily sought by birds and is often ragged from close calls. Their hyper habits make them best observed and photographed when they are basking in sunshine or puddling on muddy shores or roadsides.

▫ **Garden Nectar Plants:** shrubs: butterfly bush, bougainvillea, native azaleas; perennials: swamp milkweed, wild bergamot, lyre-leaf sage, ironweeds; biennials: native thistles, dame's rocket; annuals: pentas, tithonia, *Verbena bonariensis*, zinnias.

▫ **Garden Host Plants:** trees: plants in the citrus family; small trees: citrus, hardy orange, hoptrees, prickly-ash, Hercules' club, wild lyme, sea amyris; perennials: gas plant, garden rue. This butterfly also loves orange-jasmine, which is commonly used as a northern houseplant or summer patio plant.

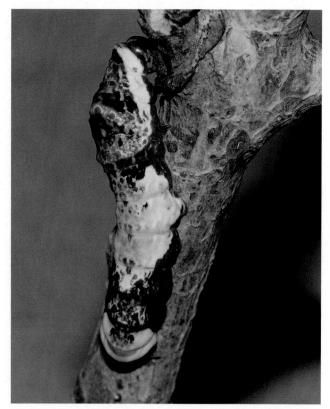

The caterpillar of the Giant Swallowtail looks like a bird dropping.

TIPS
TO ATTRACT

This butterfly can't resist two tropical annuals: If you plant Mexican sunflower and *Verbena bonariensis* you are almost assured of a visit by this swallowtail in hot-summer regions. If you want them to colonize your yard, their all-time-favorite host plants are prickly-ashes found in the South, Southwest and Midwest. Unfortunately, prickly-ashes aren't considered the most ornamental of shrubs or small trees, so plant one in that back corner of your butterfly reserve!

□ **Identification:** 4 to 6.25 inches. Unmistakably large, Giant Swallowtails are an overall rich brown with yellow bands that form an "X" in the outer forewing. These swallowtails have an easily visible yellow spot in them.

□ **Caterpillar:** A living bird dropping all its life, with a fresh, wet look. This coloration deters birds from eating it. They exude bright-red osmeteria when disturbed. Giant Swallowtails are often called orange dogs in citrus country, where they can become a pest, and colonies are purposely eradicated in citrus country.

□ **Chrysalis:** Giant Swallowtail's chrysalis is cryptic brown or gray to look like a stub on the stem or trunk where they form.

A side view of a Giant Swallowtail nectaring on a zinnia.

Swallowtails

69

Eastern Tiger Swallowtail

Papilio glaucus

Next to the Monarch, the tiger swallowtails are probably the most well known and cherished North American butterflies. We now know there are five distinct species of tiger swallowtails and that this one, the Eastern Tiger Swallowtail, is the most common and widespread.

The Eastern Tiger Swallowtail is aptly named for its yellow wings that are striped and edged in black, and for its range in the eastern half of the continent. This species is the most variable of the tiger swallowtails and changes dramatically from brood to brood. It shares turf throughout most of its range with the unpalatable Pipevine Swallowtail, and some female Eastern Tiger Swallowtails have black and blue wings that mimic it.

Eastern Tiger Swallowtails are a favorite food of many birds and often show tattered and missing wing pieces from close calls. Eastern Tiger Swallowtails have multiple broods per year—spring broods that emerge from overwintering chrysalises are smallest and canary yellow. Summer broods are much larger and duller yellow or ochre yellow. Males form spectacular puddle parties on muddy banks of forested rivers.

□ **Status:** A hardy resident butterfly, Eastern Tiger Swallowtail survives the winter as a chrysalis.

□ **Habitat:** Eastern Tiger Swallowtails are denizens of forests, woodlands, savannas and forested urban areas, most at home in the treetops. They commonly venture into adjacent meadows, grasslands and gardens in search of nectar.

□ **Garden Habit:** This familiar and favorite butterfly buoyantly glides down from the treetops to nectar on its favorite flowers. It often becomes quite docile while nectaring—wings outspread for all the world to see, as it teeters over every floret to get nectar.

□ **Garden Nectar Plants:** small trees: apples/crabapples, mimosa and plums; shrubs: abelias, butterfly bush, button-

A Canadian Tiger Swallowtail nectars on dandelions.

bush, mock oranges, native azaleas, garden lilacs; perennials: milkweeds, purple coneflowers, Joe-Pye-weed, Oriental lilies, wild bergamot, garden phlox, lyre-leaf sage, cupplant; biennials: native thistles, dame's rocket; annuals: bachelor buttons, pentas, Mexican sunflower, *Verbena bonariensis*, zinnias.

□ **Garden Host Plants:** shade trees: ashes, tulip tree, black cherry; small trees: sweetbay magnolia, native and hybrid magnolias, chokecherry.

□ **Identification:** 3 to 6.25 inches. As with all tiger swallowtails, it has bold, black stripes over yellow. Females have a beautiful blue wash on the hind wings and faded outer tips on their forewings. An outer row of yellow spots (not forming a stripe) on the edge of the forewing's underside is distinct. Orange is suffused with all of the outer spots on the underside of the hind wings. Some females are charcoal-brown-black with a blue wash on the hind wings, but the black tiger-stripe pattern is still readily visible, especially from the underside. Black females may produce yellow female offspring and vice versa. Black females are less common northeastward and absent in lower-peninsular Florida.

□ **Caterpillar:** Eastern Tiger Swallowtails begin life as a small green or brown bird-dropping look-alike to avoid predation. Older caterpillars are green with two small eyes

A dark phase, female Eastern Tiger Swallowtail nectars on dame's rocket.

A sweetbay magnolia is like manna from heaven to an Eastern Tiger Swallowtail. Any shrub lilac will attract spring broods, and old-fashioned varieties of perennial garden phlox (many new cultivars are nectarless!) are a favorite of summer broods. Plant a border of Joe-Pye-weed, *Verbena bonariensis*, and butterfly bush, with red pentas in the foreground.

and a black shoulder band. They rest on their silk-blanketed pad on the upper side of a leaf all day and feed at night. They exude forked orange osmeteria that give the caterpillar a snakehead-like appearance when disturbed.

▫ **Chrysalis:** Eastern Tiger Swallowtail's chrysalis is cryptically colored to look like a broken stub of the twig they're attached to.

▫ **Local Relative:** Canadian Tiger Swallowtail (*Papilio canadensis*). This is the tiger swallowtail of the Canadian region (including Alaska), northern Rocky Mountains and northern Great Plains.

Eastern Tiger Swallowtails love Joe-Pye-weed.

Western Tiger Swallowtail
Papilio rutulus

This is the tiger swallowtail of most of the Pacific West and central and southern Rocky Mountains. Often slighted in the literature by its bigger, dynamic cousin in the East, the Western Tiger Swallowtail deserves more, as it is a common visitor to gardens in our most populous state of California and Canada's third largest urban area, Vancouver.

Unlike the Eastern Tiger Swallowtail, whose male and female butterflies are readily differentiated, the Western Tiger Swallowtail's males and females look pretty much the same. There is only one brood of Western Tiger Swallowtails throughout most of their interior and high elevations range, two broods on the Pacific Coast and four broods present all year in sunny southern California. There is little difference in the appearance of different broods. Even though it is the western look-alike of the Eastern and Canadian Tiger Swallowtail, it is actually more closely related to the creamy white-colored Pale (tiger) Swallowtail, which rarely ventures into gardens and is described below.

□ **Status:** A hardy resident butterfly, Western Tiger Swallowtail survives the winter as a chrysalis. It is present all year in southern California.

□ **Habitat:** Western Tiger Swallowtail is a butterfly of the forests, woodlands, savannas and treed urban areas. This swallowtail, like its eastern counterpart, prefers the treetops but ventures into adjacent meadows, gardens and other open lands for nectar. Inhabiting the dry West, it prefers wooded riparian habitats, and males can form large puddle parties in muddy streamsides or other puddles.

□ **Garden Habit:** Western Tiger Swallowtails will fly high in the trees surrounding your garden and will be enticed to descend by garden flowers. It does not continually flutter, but keeps its wings outspread while it nectars. A most cordial garden visitor.

□ **Garden Nectar Plants:** small tree: California buckeye; shrubs: butterfly bush, escallonia, hibiscus, lantanas, mock oranges, rosemary, garden lilacs, Yerba Santa, California fuchsias; **perennials:** columbines, milkweeds, purple cone-

A Pale Swallowtail—the lighter close relative of the Western Tiger Swallowtail.

flower, wild buckwheats, lavender, sages, rose verbena; annuals: lantanas, Mexican sunflower.

□ **Garden Host Plants:** shade trees: white alder, ashes, California sycamore, quaking aspen, cottonwoods; small trees: water birch, black hawthorn, apples, hoptrees, bitter cherry, chokecherry, plums, willows; shrubs: Saskatoon serviceberry, willows.

□ **Identification:** 2.5 to 3.75 inches. The most common western "tiger swallowtail" does not associate with Canadian Tiger Swallowtail where they can be found together in British Columbia, Washington, Idaho, Montana. Like the Canadian Tiger Swallowtail, there is a yellow stripe on the outer edge of the forewing's underside. There is, however, no orange suffused with yellow spots on the outer edges of the hind wing's underside which Eastern and Canadian Swallowtails display.

□ **Caterpillar:** Caterpillars are bright

Two Western Tiger Swallowtails nectar on wild phlox.

TIPS
TO ATTRACT

Plant a native or garden mock orange. Western Tiger Swallowtails love to nectar on the sweet-scented blossoms of this late-spring-blooming shrub. Plant a flower border of butterfly bush underplanted with lantanas. If natives are your game, then a rock garden with Yerba Santa, wild buck-wheats, your favorite native sage and California fuchsia is sure to please this swallowtail.

green with two fake eye spots and a black and yellow band at their shoulders. They reside during the day in a shelter created by drawing leaves together with their own silken strands. They venture out to feed at night.

□ **Chrysalis:** Western Tiger Swallowtail's chrysalis is cryptic brown and gray with a distinct darker line down the mid-dle of its sides. It looks very much like a twig stub, just like the other tiger swallowtails'.

□ **Local Relative:** Pale Swallowtail (*Papilio eurymedon*) is a tiger swallowtail that is cream-colored instead of yellow. This butterfly is an uncommon denizen of gardens unless you live on the edge of its knoll, ridge and mountaintop habitat.

A Western Tiger Swallowtail basks on a vine maple leaf.

Two-Tailed Swallowtail

Papilio multicaudata

Show any kindergartner this butterfly and ask how many tails it has; and the answer will be four. The Latin name means multiple-tailed butterfly, which would be a better name, since this swallowtail has two tails on *each* of its hind wings. The inner two are shorter and the outer two longer. It was formerly called the Two-Tailed Tiger Swallowtail, which is also appropriate, as this swal-

A Two-Tailed Swallowtail nectars on a wild thistle.

lowtail has the typical yellow with black tiger-striped pattern found on three other swallowtails with tiger in their name.

The Two-Tailed Swallowtail rivals the Eastern Tiger Swallowtail and Giant Swallowtail as North America's largest butterfly. It is the largest butterfly where it is found. It acts like the other tiger swallowtails and is most at home in the treetops of forests or open woodlands but will readily venture down for puddling, nectaring and egg laying. Though seldom common, they readily visit gardens and have expanded in range and population as one of their favorite host plants, green ash, has been commonly planted as a street tree in western cities and suburbs. This butterfly may also be expanding its range eastward into the Great Plains where towns and streambeds that were once short-grass prairie now support shade tree oases.

▫ **Status:** Two-Tailed Swallowtail is a hardy resident butterfly that overwinters as a chrysalis. It colonizes or strays eastward into the western Great Plains.

▫ **Habitat:** This tiger swallowtail inhabits drier mountains and hills than its counterparts. In California, for example, it lives either on the drier, desert-facing sides of mountains or on the mountains in the desert. Even in its drier habitats, it is most common in woodlands of moist canyons among

semi-arid, mid-elevation mountains and foothills. Two-Tailed Swallowtail has also adapted to our human landscape and is prevalent in urban areas and suburbs, such as Denver and its suburbs.

▫ **Garden Habit:** Two-Tailed Swallowtails fly high in the trees surrounding your garden and will be enticed to descend by their favorite garden flowers. Like all tiger swallowtails, they don't continually flutter while they nectar—they keep their wings outspread, showing off their status as the most beautiful of the tiger swallowtails.

▫ **Garden Nectar Plants:** small trees: Texas madrone, desert-willow; shrubs: manzanitas, butterfly bush, woolly butterfly bush, claret-cup cactus, California fuchsias; perennials: milkweeds, cardinal flower, monkeyflowers, monardellas, penstemons, scabiosas; annuals: bloodflower, Mexican sunflower, *Verbena bonariensis*, zinnias.

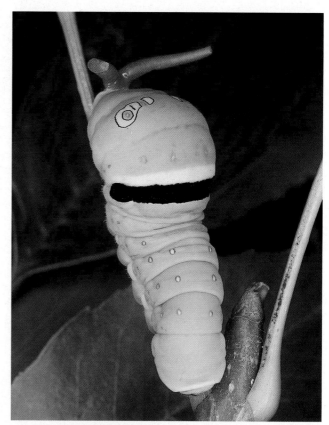

A Two-Tailed Swallowtail caterpillar.

▫ **Garden Host Plants:** shade trees: velvet ash, green ash, California sycamore; shrubs: chokecherry, hoptrees.

▫ **Identification:** 2.75 to 6.0 inches. A Tiger Swallowtail of the typical yellow-and-black-striped pattern but the stripes are the narrowest of the four species. Two-Tailed Swallowtails are the only swallowtail with two tails on each hind

Plant a velvet ash or green ash as a shade tree—this butterfly prefers these two trees as host plants. If you don't have space for a shade tree, then any of the native hoptree shrubs will do just fine, but they are not readily available from nurseries. Xeriscaping is common in most of this butterfly's range, so plant claret-cup cactus, California fuchsia and butterflyweed, all of which are exceedingly drought tolerant.

wing. The females are the most colorful, their base color noticeably orange-yellow, their stripes wider, and they display more blue wash on their hind wings. Two-Tailed Swallowtail is the largest of the western swallowtails with a wingspan approaching 6 inches.

❑ **Caterpillar:** Two-Tailed Swallowtail caterpillars are nearly identical to other tiger swallowtails but have smaller fake eyes and are apple green. The caterpillars fold leaves over themselves to create a protective nest, as does the Spicebush Swallowtail in the East. The caterpillar becomes reddish before forming a chrysalis.

❑ **Chrysalis:** Two-Tailed Swallowtail's chrysalis looks very much like a twig stub, just like the other tiger swallowtails.

A Two-Tailed Swallowtail nectars on a showy milkweed blossom.

Spicebush Swallowtail

Papilio troilus

Spicebush Swallowtail is the third major swallowtail named for its host plant, though the butterfly's caterpillars will eat several other related plants.

The butterfly's old name of "Green-Clouded Swallowtail" should be resurrected, since the butterfly has an outer row of trendy sage-green spots along the margin of its hind wings. Male butterflies have additional iridescent green clouding dusted across their entire hind wings. Female butterflies' hind wings are dusted with iridescent blue to mimic the distasteful Pipevine Swallowtail.

The Spicebush Swallowtail could also be named for its roaming lifestyle. Though its range is limited to places where its host plants—spicebush, sassafras and camphor—are found, it seems to roam in all directions. It commonly strays up the Mississippi River Valley, out into the Great Plains and even across the Strait of Florida to Cuba.

Sassafras is a great host plant for the Spicebush Swallowtail.

A female Spicebush Swallowtail nectars on butterfly milkweed.

▫ **Status:** Spicebush Swallowtail is a hardy resident butterfly that overwinters as a chrysalis. It can show up as a stray in all directions.

▫ **Habitat:** Spicebush Swallowtails reside in forest, woodlands, savannas and wooded urban areas. They venture into adjacent grasslands, marshes and beyond in search of nectar. Males puddle at woodland streamsides and puddles. They are commonly found in gardens, as they have an exceptional sweet tooth for nectar-rich garden flowers.

▫ **Garden Habit:** Spicebush Swallowtails always act a bit hurried. Females are especially fluttery (like a Pipevine Swallowtail, which they mimic). Once they find a favorite nectar source they often become docile and show off their outspread wings.

▫ **Garden Nectar Plants:** Spicebush Swallowtails have a long proboscis and can readily visit long-tubed flowers often reserved for hummingbirds, including: small tree: mimosa; shrubs: butterfly bush, summersweet clethra, native azaleas; perennials: butterflyweed and other milkweeds, Joe-Pye-weed, blazingstars, bergamots, lyre-leaf sage; biennial: native thistles; annuals: jewelweeds, lantana, tropical sage, zinnias.

▫ **Garden Host Plants:** shade tree: sassafras; evergreen tree: camphor tree; shrub: spicebush.

▫ **Identification:** 3.5 to 5 inches. Spicebush Swallowtails are another large, black, sexually dimorphic butterfly. Males have a gorgeous and unmistakable sea- or sage-green wash over their hind wings and a row of similarly colored marginal spots. Females mimic Pipevine Swallowtails and have a blue wash but still have the outer row of sage-green spots. Dark female Eastern Tiger Swallowtails are similar but have the tiger-striped highlights. Female Black Swallowtails are most similar but have a pupil in the fake eyes by their tails and have two complete rows of marginal spots on the upper side of their forewing.

▫ **Caterpillars:** Spicebush Swallowtail has the spookiest caterpillar. Apple green above, brown below, with large fake eyes on the shoulders, it looks like a snake—especially

A Spicebush Swallowtail caterpillar turns brown prior to forming a chrysalis.

If you plant a sassafras tree or a spicebush, the Spicebush Swallowtail will come and find you! An annual bed of large single zinnias, plus 'Lady in Red', 'Coral Nymph' and 'Snow Nymph' salvias (tropical sage), edged with yellow and orange lantanas, is also sure to please them. A perennial border of milkweeds, bergamot, blazingstars and Joe-Pye-weed will readily bring these swallowtails to native-themed gardens.

when it is disturbed and it shoots out its tongue-like, bright-yellow forked osmeterium. Young instars are bird-dropping-like green or gray with a brown splotch on their white rear end. The caterpillar nests by spinning a silk pad on a leaf and folding both leaf edges over itself. There it resides all day and ventures out to feed at night. These curled-leaf nests make the caterpillars easy for gardeners to locate on their food plants.

□ **Chrysalis:** Spicebush Swallowtail's chrysalis mimics a leaf—either live green or dead brown, with a prominent ridge and line down its middle, just like a leaf's midvein. The chrysalis' camouflage helps hide it from hungry birds and other predators.

A male Spicebush Swallowtail nectars on a goldflame honeysuckle blossom.

Swallowtails

Palamedes Swallowtail
Papilio palamedes

Palamedes Swallowtail is another mythologically named swallowtail. Palamedes was the son of Nauplius, King of Euboea—the large Greek island in the Aegean Sea. An old name for this butterfly is "Magnolia Swallowtail," for it is often found in deep-South forests and gardens wherever the magnificent evergreen southern magnolias are found.

A Palamedes Swallowtail rests under a leaf.

Palamedes Swallowtails are closely associated with southern swamps of bald cypress festooned in Spanish moss, and flatwoods of open long-leaf and slash pines that are carpeted with wiregrass and wildflowers. From Virginia's Great Dismal Swamp to Texas's Big Thicket, these southern coastal plain habitats are dotted with groves of this swallowtail's host plant, the redbays. Redbays are evergreen shrubs and trees in the laurel family and their closest well-known relative is the tropical avocado, which the Palamedes Swallowtail's caterpillar will eat where it is cultivated in southern Florida. The host plant's limited range in the deep South and Florida keep this butterfly at home only in southern gardens.

▫ **Status:** Palamedes Swallowtail is a hardy resident butterfly that overwinters as a chrysalis. It has, but only a few times, strayed northward up the Atlantic coast to Long Island and northwestward all the way to Nebraska!

▫ **Habitat:** Palamedes Swallowtails inhabit forested wetlands, swamps and flatwoods and venture into nearby meadows and marshes in search of nectar. Males can congregate at puddles and muddy shorelines by the hundreds. They readily visit gardens and are probably the most common swallowtail in Florida.

▫ **Garden Habit:** Palamedes Swallowtails wander slowly through woods and forest edges, seldom flying higher than head height. They flutter nearly continually but can become docile once enamored of their favorite nectar sources.

▫ **Garden Nectar Plants:** shrubs: summersweet clethra, native azaleas; perennials: *Verbena bonariensis*, columbine, lyre-leaf sage, pickerel weed, southern wild irises and their hybrid "Louisiana" irises; biennial: native thistles; annual: lantanas (a perennial along the coast and shrub in Florida).

▫ **Garden Host Plants:** small trees: rarely cultivated redbay, which is available only at nurseries that specialize in native plants, and avocado in tropical south Florida.

▫ **Identification:** 4.5 to 5.25 inches. Palamedes Swallowtail is a large, dark chocolate brown swallowtail with yellow bands and marginal spotting. There is a distinctive yellow

The foliage of the redbay provides food for the Palamedes Swallowtail caterpillar.

stripe at the base of the hind wing's underside. Its closest relative is the Spicebush Swallowtail, and they will occasionally court one another.

▫ **Caterpillar:** Palamedes Swallowtail caterpillars are nearly identical to Spicebush Swallowtail caterpillars but the bird-

TIPS
TO ATTRACT

Plant a water garden filled with pickerel weed, southern "Louisiana" irises and a redbay on its bank. Leave a part of the lawn unmowed in spring for the weedy wild perennial salvia, lyre-leaf sage, to flower and provide nectar. Plant a flower border of blue *Verbena bonariensis* fronted by orange and gold lantanas.

dropping-like young caterpillars have a nearly all-white rear end. Mature caterpillars are hump-backed and pale green above and reddish brown below. Caterpillars turn pale yellow prior to forming a chrysalis. Palamedes Swallowtail caterpillars live exposed on new foliage of the host plants and do not roll the leaves over them as do Spicebush Swallowtail caterpillars.

▫ **Chrysalis:** Palamedes Swallowtail's chrysalis mimics a leaf—either live green or dead brown with a prominent ridge and line down its middle, just like a leaf's midvein. The chrysalis's camouflage helps hide it from hungry birds and other predators.

A Palamedes Swallowtail nectars on pentas with its wings outspread.

WHITES & SULPHURS

*W*hites and sulphurs are abundant butterflies across the entire continent. They come in three primary colors—white, yellow and orange—and are active fliers in the garden. They literally sparkle as they flutter about. One of their kind, the Yellow European Sulphur, called the Brimstone, originated the English name "butterfly," which is short for "butter-colored fly." The chrysalises of whites and sulphurs contain a silken thread around their middle, which helps fasten them to a stem or leaf.

Checkered White

Pontia protodice

Checkered Whites are the original common white butterfly that populates most of North America by summer's end. They are sexually dimorphic (the males and females look different). The females have a more dramatic dark-checkered pattern to their white wings, which gives this butterfly its name, while males have only some remnant spots on their forewings and have hind wings that are nearly pure white.

Checkered Whites were once more common (they can still have occasional population explosions in the Southwest), but they have lost ground where non-native Cabbage Whites are abundant. The alien Cabbage Whites are more aggressive and often attack Checkered Whites.

The native Checkered White feeds on plants in the same family as the Cabbage White but rarely eats cabbages and other vegetables, so they are not considered a pest species like the Cabbage White. Checkered Whites like to eat the plants that we assume are weeds, so we spray and pull the plants required to keep the Checkered White in our landscapes. Their urban host plants thrive in neglected places; thus, Checkered Whites have learned to live on the wrong side of the tracks, so to speak. Checkered Whites are also more at home in native grassland habitats, while the Cabbage White prefers the irrigated, coddled landscape most of us call home. Courtship in Checkered Whites is unique in that males may chase females or females may chase males.

□ **Status:** Checkered Whites are a resident butterfly that overwinters as a chrysalis or as a colonist in northern regions—the exact zone between resident and colonist butterflies is unknown and may change depending on the severity of winter's weather.

□ **Habitat:** Checkered Whites inhabit prairies, meadows, pastures, fallow fields, disturbed vacant lots and other waste areas.

□ **Garden Habitat:** Checkered Whites will visit butterfly gardens on occasion, usually later in the season. If you have a lot of Cabbage Whites around, you will seldom have a Checkered White. In inner city areas, dry western and coastal regions, the Checkered White can be more prevalent.

□ **Garden Nectar Plants:** perennials: asters, blazingstars, milkweeds; weedy plants: winter cress and mustards.

□ **Garden Host Plants:** flowers and fruit of weedy plants in the mustard family like peppergrass (which looks great in dried arrangements), shepherd's purse and winter cress.

□ **Identification:** 1.75 to 2.5 inches. Female Checkered Whites are aptly named and display the checkered pattern of dark gray on white on their open forewings. Males are whiter with four spots on their forewing and several spots along their wing apex (tip of the wing).

The underside of a male Checkered White.

By planting native wildflowers found in dry grassland or desert habitats of your region, you are likely to attract the Checkered White. Plant several species of summer-blooming blazingstars and several species of fall-blooming wild asters to provide a continuous bloom and a plentiful supply of nectar.

◻ **Caterpillar:** The caterpillar is slate gray with black speckling and yellow or orange-yellow stripes.

◻ **Chrysalis:** The chrysalis is slate gray with thorn-like projections on its head and back.

◻ **Local Relative:** Western White (*Pontia occidentalis*) is nearly identical and common in the northwestern one-third of the continent—it can best be identified by its dark abdomen. Checkered Whites' abdomens are white or white dusted.

A male Checkered White nectars on wild asters.

Whites & Sulphurs

Cabbage White
Pieris rapae

Cabbage Whites are our most abundant introduced butterfly. Their old name, European Cabbage Butterfly, is appropriate, as they were introduced to Quebec from Europe around 1860. In 20 years, Cabbage Whites presided over most of the eastern half of the continent. Today they range from coast to coast with only a few semitropical and desert regions where they are uncommon or absent.

The starling of the butterfly world, Cabbage Whites are no more alien than most of us and they really add some color and life to the butterfly garden. Their bright-white wings add another hue to the other butterflies fluttering about a garden, and they are active from early in the season until late in the fall. In the middle part of the country, they are present from March to November and are found all year in the deep South and California.

If you are a vegetable gardener, Cabbage Whites are one of your worst enemies: pests to cabbages and related plants. Plant cleome and nasturtium flowers to provide host plants, and cage your choice vegetables. If you use Bt dust to control Cabbage Whites on your vegetables, be careful that it does not blow onto adjacent host plants and harm other species. This ubiquitous butterfly, which lays about 700 eggs per female, is impossible to eradicate and you will certainly eliminate many desirable butterflies by blanket spraying chemicals anywhere beyond the veggies that it threatens.

❑ **Status:** Cabbage Whites are a resident butterfly that overwinters as a chrysalis.

❑ **Habitat:** Cabbage Whites are common in yards and gardens, fields and pastures. They are uncommon or absent from the dry habitats that Checkered Whites favor.

❑ **Garden Habit:** Cabbage Whites actively fly about the garden and nectar on a variety of plants that many other butterflies seldom visit. They definitely prefer flowers with blue, purple and yellow tones.

❑ **Garden Nectar Plants:** shrub: butterfly bush; perennials: asters, mints, bergamots, goldenrods, red clover, vervains; annuals: bog salvia, *Verbena bonariensis;* and weedy plants: mustards, winter cress, dogbane and dandelions.

❑ **Garden Host Plants:** cleome, nasturtiums, pests on garden cabbage, collards, broccoli, radishes, etc.; weedy plants: mustard, peppergrass and winter cress and other weeds in the mustard family.

❑ **Identification:** 1.75 to 2.25 inches. Cabbage Whites are a medium-sized, bright-white butterfly with dark wing

A Cabbage White, an import from Europe, nectars on another European import—perennial salvia.

TIPS
TO ATTRACT

A tip to attract this pest species will no doubt turn the stomach of vegetable gardeners, but will lure Cabbage Whites away from your prized vegetables: Plant self-sowing annual cleome or plant nasturtiums, which are an annual in the North and perennial in mild regions where the butterfly is already present. Enjoy the native Checkered White in areas where this butterfly is absent.

tips and one spot on the forewing of males and two spots on the forewing of females.

□ **Caterpillar:** The caterpillar is green with minute black dots and a yellow dashed line down each side. It is the pesky "worm" on your cabbages.

□ **Chrysalis:** The chrysalis is either green or brown with pointed projections on its head and back.

□ **Local Relative:** Great Southern White (*Ascia monuste*) is common near the beach in Florida and along the Gulf Coast—and rarely strays inland as far as the northern Great Plains. It is a medium-large white butterfly with phosphorescent blue antennae tips.

White on white: A Cabbage White nectars on boltonia.

Orangetips

Anthocharis spp.

Orangetips are butterflies of the spring but, unfortunately, few of us have ever noticed their springtime flight among the wild plums and redbuds. The name orangetip is obvious, but female Falcate Orangetips (*Anthocharis midea*) lack the characteristic orange tips (apex) of the wings. It is notable that orangetips are the longest-lived butterflies. The eastern Falcate Orangetip often doesn't hatch from its chrysalis the following spring

A Pacific Orangetip nectars on a forget-me-not flower—showing off its marbled underside.

but waits an additional year. The Desert Orangetip (*Euchloe cethura*) of southwestern deserts may not hatch from its chrysalis for up to six years! These are adaptations to emerge when spring flowers are at their prime, and droughty, flowerless years are avoided.

The western Sara Orangetip is the most widespread and frequently encountered species and has now been divided into four nearly identical species. We can thank scientists and their new methods of chemical analysis that confirm this—but how each one lived a different life should have given us a clue. The four new species are: Pacific Orangetip (*Anthocharis sara*), Southern Rocky Mountain Orangetip (*A. julia*), Stella Orangetip (*A. stella*), and Southwestern Orangetip (*A. thoosa*). The days of identifying and classifying animals based on dead museum specimens has expanded into the field where observing the live animals in their habitat and going about their day-to-day existence is the norm.

▫ **Status:** Orangetips are resident butterflies that overwinter as a chrysalis.

▫ **Habitat:** Pacific Orangetips reside in woodlands and foothill valleys and canyons where its flight follows streamsides; Southern Rocky Mountain Orangetips in ponderosa and lodgepole pine forests; Stella Orangetips in montane

forests and adjacent meadows; and Southwestern Orangetips in pinyon and juniper woodlands. Desert Orangetips are found in desert hills and ridges. Falcate Orangetips are encountered in open woodlands or savannas and young lowland woods. All orangetips will inhabit these habitats among urban development but are generally absent from dense urban areas, dense forests and treeless or shrubless grasslands and deserts.

▫ **Garden Habit:** Orangetips will visit your garden only if you are adjacent to wild areas and corridors of natural habitat. A lot of new suburban development in the Southeast and West qualifies. They usually just patrol through the yard in search of a mate and will stop only briefly to nectar if you have some of their tiny vernal nectar plants.

▫ **Garden Nectar Plants:** small tree: wild plums; perennials: rock cresses, wild strawberries, violets; weedy plants: winter cress, tansy mustards.

▫ **Garden Host Plants:** rock cresses and other related plants in the mustard family.

Horned violet makes a great nectar plant for orangetips.

Maintain natural buffer areas between you and your neighbors. Do not mow your entire property! Support protection of open spaces and greenways in your neighborhood. Plant rock cresses and violets, or cherish the wild ones already there. Plant patches of wild plums or redbuds along the outer portions of your property.

□ **Identification:** 1.5 to 2 inches. Tiny white butterflies with an orange-sherbet-colored splotch near the forewing apex or tip. When they perch with their wings closed, they display marbling of greenish and/or grayish tones. It is easiest to identify an orangetip species by location and habitat—otherwise just enjoy their special beauty as another one of those things that make springtime so special.

□ **Caterpillar:** The green caterpillars will only eat the flowers and fruit of their host plants.

□ **Chrysalis:** The tiny chrysalis has a long, cone-like head and is usually colored dark green to brown to match its surroundings.

A Pacific Orangetip rests on a forget-me-not.

Whites & Sulphurs

Clouded Sulphur & Orange Sulphur

Colias philodice and *Colias eurytheme*

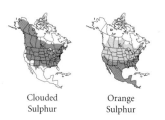

Clouded
Sulphur

Orange
Sulphur

These two ubiquitous lemon-yellow and melon-orange colored butterflies are found across much of the continent. Well known by gardeners, they frequent urban and suburban landscapes but fly together in greatest abundance over hayfields that contain both their nectar and host plants.

Clouded and Orange Sulphurs have almost exactly the same patterns on their wings—only their coloration differs, which is even more distinct as seen through their ultraviolet-sensitive eyes. The yellow Clouded Sulphur absorbs ultraviolet light, and the melon-colored Orange Sulphur reflects ultraviolet light—giving it a glossy look in their eyes. Female butterflies are larger and have spotting in their dark wing margins. A few females of both species are white with a bluish tinge to them. Only they know which white female species is which, as they are identical in our eyes, but the two species do occasionally hybridize.

The Orange Sulphur's old name was Alfalfa Butterfly—named for its favorite host plant, as this butterfly can become a pest in alfalfa fields. Orange Sulphurs were at one time found only in central and western North America but around 1890 they colonized eastern regions and are now found almost everywhere. They are generally more common in the South and colonize northern regions. Clouded Sulphurs are generally more common in the North and absent from the deep South. Most American gardeners host both species in their gardens.

□ **Status:** Clouded Sulphur is a resident throughout its

range; Orange Sulphur cannot survive severe winters and is a resident in the South and West and a colonist elsewhere.
□ **Habitat:** Both sulphurs thrive in hayfields, meadows, native grasslands, open woodlands, roadsides, lawns and gardens.
□ **Garden Habit:** Clouded and Orange Sulphurs usually beeline into the garden in a low, hurried flight. They stop in the lawn if you've allowed clover to be a part of it—they nectar and lay eggs on white clover. They hurriedly investi-

An Orange Sulphur shows off its canteloupe-colored upperside.

gate garden flower borders and stop to nectar on their favorite flowers.
□ **Garden Nectar Plants:** perennials: milkweeds, asters, blazingstars, goldenrods, clovers, vervains; annual: marigolds; weedy plants: dandelions, winter cress, dogbane, clovers.
□ **Garden Host Plants:** perennial: alfalfa (favored by Orange Sulphur); weedy plants: sweet clovers, white clover (favored by Clouded Sulphur), vetches.
□ **Identification:** 2 to 2.75 inches. Clouded Sulphurs are medium-sized sulphurs that are yellow with black marginal bands. Orange Sulphurs (2 to 3 inches) are the same except they are melon-orange colored. Both females have spots in their forewing marginal bands and a more broken hind wing marginal band. Female Orange Sulphurs are not so evenly colored as the males—they are just blushed with melon-orange.
□ **Caterpillar:** Both species have identical caterpillars and chrysalises. The caterpillar is green with a lighter band

A male Clouded Sulphur perches on a lantana blossom.

The Gardener's Butterfly Book

Plant white clover in your lawn, or maintain existing stands of clover. Plant a garden border of single marigolds, these sulphurs' favorite nationwide garden flower to nectar on.

down its back and bands of white with a rosy line in the middle down each side.

❑ **Chrysalis:** The chrysalis is green and mottled cream and black with a yellow band down its side.

❑ **Local Relatives:** There are many very similar, related species found in the far North where the Pink-Edged Sulphur is most common and in high elevations out West where Queen Alexandra's Sulphur is most common. These sulphur relatives are seldom found in gardens.

The Clouded Sulphur, usually predominantly yellow, can take on a green tinge. This one is a female.

Southern Dogface

Zerene cesonia

What a name for a pretty butterfly! The Southern Dogface's upper side forewing patterns draw a most interesting picture. The outline of a poodle's head defined between the yellow wing and its black margins is unmistakable, and the butterfly's forewing cell spot becomes the fake dog's eye. The female butterfly's pattern is less distinct. From the side, a vague outline of this pattern is readily seen through the wing while the butterfly nectars—always with its wings closed. Unfortunately, the full, striking pattern is not seen unless the butterfly is killed because it only opens its wings when in flight. Any Southern Dogface with open wings on a garden flower is probably in the lethal clutches of a crab spider!

The "Southern" portion of its name is also very accurate because this butterfly is a denizen of hot-summer places. From Argentina into the Gulf Coast of the United States, this butterfly resides year-round. In summer it spreads northward with the heat, colonizing much of the Southwest, Midwest, South and coastal areas of the East. Fall butterflies display a rich pink hue to the underside of their yellow hind wings, making them one of the most beautiful autumnal butterflies. Wherever there is a hard freeze, this butterfly is killed and won't return until emigrants from frost-free zones replace it the following season.

□ **Status:** Southern Dogface is a resident only in Florida, Gulf Coast regions (during mild winters) and southeast Arizona, where it overwinters as an adult butterfly. Dogfaces colonize hot summer regions elsewhere.

□ **Habitat:** Southern Dogfaces favor dry, short grassland habitats, including dunescapes, various scrub habitats, deserts; sandy, gravelly or hilly prairies; dry, weedy pastures; and open woodlands or savannas.

□ **Garden Habit:** Southern Dogfaces are active in the garden as they fly between flowers to nectar on. They never open their wings while nectaring.

□ **Garden Nectar Plants:** perennials: asters, coreopsis, alfalfa, vervains.

□ **Garden Host Plants:** shrubs: indigobush, leadplant; perennials: daleas and prairie clovers, clovers; crops: soybeans, alfalfa.

□ **Identification:** 2.25 to 3 inches. Southern Dogface is a medium-yellow sulphur with the distinctive poodle head silhouette in the forewings visible even when the wings are closed. Females have a more hook-tipped forewing and a less distinctive poodle-head field mark. Fall butterflies tout a rich pink cast to the underside of their hind wings.

□ **Caterpillar:** The variably light or dark caterpillars are black-dotted yellow-green with a pale band on each side, which contains orange dashes.

This is the typical garden view of a live Southern Dogface—they never open their wings except in flight.

You can entice a Southern Dogface into your garden if you live near appropriate habitat and plant their favorite sources of nectar: coreopsis and perennial asters. Plant purple prairie clover, which is both a host plant and a spectacularly colored, long-lived, native perennial too.

□ **Chrysalis:** The chrysalis is bluish green with a gray line along its side.
□ **Local Relative:** California Dogface (*Zerene eurydice*) "flying pansy."

Males have a yellow-orange-colored poodle head that has an outrageous violet cast to it. Females are pure yellow with hooked wing tips. Together they are the official state insect of California.

A mounted Southern Dogface specimen shows off the dogface pattern on its forewings.

Whites & Sulphurs

Cloudless Sulphur

Phoebis sennae

Cloudless Sulphurs are flying sunshine. Their brilliant yellow wings transport a bit of the tropics to warm temperate regions. Emigrating northward up major rivers and warm coastlines, the Cloudless Sulphur colonizes the warmest southern third of the United States each year and strays much beyond—all the way to Canada on occasion. The new immigrants from the south lay eggs on annual partridge peas and perennial sennas and within a month their offspring are flying about too.

Cloudless Sulphurs have some traits shared by hummingbirds: a long tongue (proboscis), a sweet tooth and a passion for red flowers. Unfortunately, they don't seem to grasp the use of nectar feeders, which the birds have mastered.

When cold weather arrives in fall, the Cloudless Sulphurs just hunker down, camouflaged in some yellowing foliage and wait for another warm sunny day to venture out into the garden to sip nectar. A severe freeze kills them. Unlike the migratory Monarch (or the hummingbird), which migrates south for the winter, most Cloudless Sulphurs die when summer does. In some regions, masses of Cloudless Sulphurs move southward in fall.

When spring returns, those that survived in mild Floridian and Gulf Coast regions, as well as those from the tropics, move northward once again. A mild winter brings them back quicker and in larger numbers.

▫ **Status:** Cloudless Sulphurs are a resident butterfly in semitropical regions and a colonist in the hot-summer southern third of the continent—strays can show up about anywhere.

▫ **Habitat:** A tropical butterfly of almost any sunny space, including open woods, savannas, grasslands and disturbed areas like roadsides, parks, yards and gardens.

▫ **Garden Habit:** Cloudless Sulphurs mass around their favorite nectar flowers and move around the garden from late morning to afternoon, to those flowers that bask in the most sunshine of the hour. They are the quintessential garden butterfly.

The diagonal line across the closed wings of this large sulphur identify it as a Large Orange Sulphur—a close relative of the Cloudless Sulphur. The Large Orange is found mainly in the tropics.

▫ **Garden Nectar Plants:** tropical small trees/shrubs/pot plants/annuals northward: bougainvillea, hibiscus, geiger tree; shrub: autumn sage; vine: morning glories; perennials: gerberia, cardinalflower, turk's turban; annuals: impatiens, shrimp plant, species cannas, petunias, tropical sage, salvias, Mexican bush sage, coral porterweed, vinca.

▫ **Garden Host Plants:** shrub: tropical cassias; perennials: wild sennas; annuals: partridge pea, candle plant.

▫ **Identification:** 2.5 to 3.25 inches. A large lemon-yellow sulphur that is unmistakable. There are no black or dark brown margins or spots anywhere on the wings—they are *cloudless*. While nectaring with their wings closed, males appear green-yellow, females are yellow (rarely white) with a cell spot in the center of each wing with irregular light golden brown smudge spots.

▫ **Caterpillar:** Cloudless Sulphur caterpillars can be green or yellow to match their host flowers and have porcelain blue highlights.

▫ **Chrysalis:** The green or pink chrysalis is thin with a long, pointed head and big beer belly

A Cloudless Sulphur hides amongst autumn foliage and waits for a warm Indian summer day to fly again.

TIPS

TO ATTRACT

Plant a border of their favorite annual vinca; Cloudless Sulphurs are not picky about the color of them. Plant old-fashioned, single-flowered cannas for a tropical backdrop to a garden or summer screen. A patch of their host plants, either perennial sennas or annual partridge pea, is sure to lure emigrating Cloudless Sulphurs and entice a flock of them to reside in your yard and to stay through fall.

(which is actually the extended cases of the future wings). The fat, flattened look makes it look leaf-like.

▫ **Local Relatives:** Orange-Barred Sulphur (*Phoebis philea*) and Large Orange Sulphur (*P. agarithe*) are similar giant sulphurs commonly found in peninsular Florida and south Texas gardens, which will be familiar to retirees and snowbirds.

A Cloudless Sulphur visits a favorite red zinnia.

Little Yellow

Eurema lisa

The tiny, delightful and succinctly named Little Yellow is sure to visit most butterfly gardens in the eastern United States—quite a feat for such a small creature that cannot survive a cold winter in any of its forms of metamorphosis. They almost appear to spontaneously generate because undamaged butterflies can appear as early as late spring as far north as the upper Midwest. Little Yellows' direct, low-to-the-ground flight must be assisted by the winds to help them cover such an amazing distance. In fact, millions of emigrant Little Yellows have been seen flying over the Caribbean Sea and the Atlantic Ocean—they frequently colonize Bermuda. They are present in gardens most of the year in mild coastal regions and all year in Florida gardens.

Little Yellows are about the size of a quarter with their wings open, and you'll see them with their wings open only when they're in flight. Their small size makes their metamorphosis period from egg to adult very short, so a new generation is produced quickly. Little Yellows' lemon-yellow wings' uppersides are rimmed with dark brownish black, and this pattern and coloration is apparent in flight.

As with so many of the sulphurs, some females are a pale, creamy white with umber-brown edges. Otherwise the males and females appear the same to us, but the males actually reflect ultraviolet light, so male butterflies avoid butterflies that reflect. Males sip moisture from mud and form puddle parties.

▫ **Status:** Little Yellow is a resident butterfly only in the deep South and Florida, where adult butterflies overwinter. Little Yellow is a colonist in much of the United States east of the Great Plains from summer through fall.

▫ **Habitat:** Little Yellows thrive in open woods and savannas, meadows, roadsides, old fields and other sunny grasslands with flowers.

▫ **Garden Habit:** Little Yellows always seem to be just passing through, and a butterfly that stops to nectar on asters or zinnias only stops by briefly before moving on.

▫ **Garden Nectar Plants:** perennials: asters, goldenrods; annual: zinnias.

▫ **Garden Host Plants:** annual: partridge pea.

▫ **Identification:** 1.25 to 2 inches. A small sulphur, about the size of a nickel with its wings closed. When resting, it looks uniformly yellow with a few gray-brown smudges that are more extensive in females. Two tiny black spots can be seen at the base of the hind wing for a positive ID in south Florida and south Texas, where similar species of small sulphurs may occur.

▫ **Caterpillar:** The green caterpillar is dotted with tiny white spots and has a

The Mexican Yellow is a close relative of the Little Yellow and is most commonly found in the Southwest.

Plant a patch of the native annual partridge pea. Partridge pea reseeds on its own once you plant it and requires full sun and good drainage to thrive. You also will attract Cloudless Sulphur, Sleepy Orange and Gray Hairstreaks with a healthy patch of partridge pea. The caterpillars of all these butterflies will eat the flowers first, then munch the foliage down to stalks if you don't plant enough of them.

dark-green line down its back and a white or pale-green line down its sides.

□ **Chrysalis:** The green chrysalis is black dotted, with the characteristic pointed head of sulphur—it has only a small "belly" (wing cases).

□ **Local Relatives:** Barred Yellow (*Eurema daira*), which is gray dusty yellow in summer and rust-dusted yellow in winter is common in Florida gardens and a very rare stray in the Southwest and southern Great Plains.

Mexican Yellow (*E. mexicana*), which has a pointed hind wing, also strays throughout the Southwest, western Midwest and into Saskatchewan and Manitoba more than 1,000 miles from its host plants!

A Little Yellow nectars on a wild aster.

Sleepy Orange

Eurema nicippe

This senna will bloom in the heat of summer and attract nectaring Sleepy Oranges.

A perky, bright melon-orange, fast-flying butterfly—you would be hard-pressed to call this species of butterfly "sleepy." In late fall, however, one of these butterflies with a copper-colored dusting to its closed wings could be called "sleepy" because it usually rests in a shaded, protected area to overwinter and is seldom active.

The real reason this butterfly is called "sleepy" is that it lacks the eye spots that so many of the other medium-sized sulphurs have! Its eyes are closed—"sleepy," so to speak. The Latin name of this butterfly is of classical origins that has nothing to do with the butterfly. Nicippe was a Roman poet of short satires. Go figure!

Sleepy Oranges are another butterfly of summer heat and are most common in hot summer regions. Their fast-flying, straying nature has also earned them the name "rambling orange." They readily stray northward in summer—always a joyous occasion to observe in upper Midwest gardens, where a sighting of two of these butterflies in 10 summers can be expected. Their melon-orange color is very similar to the Orange Sulphur but does not reflect ultraviolet like the Orange Sulphur does, so the two look completely different in butterfly eyes.

□ **Status:** A resident in the deep South where the "sleepy" winter form of adult butterflies overwinter. Sleepy Oranges colonize the lower Midwest, southern Appalachians, mid Atlantic and Southwest. They stray a bit beyond these zones into coastal New England and the upper Midwest.

□ **Habitat:** Sleepy Oranges prefer open woods and savannas, roadsides and other woodland-edge-type habitats. They frequently visit gardens.

□ **Garden Habit:** Sleepy Oranges frequently visit gardens for nectar but never stay for long before moving on—they are actually just males patroling for females or females looking for a place to lay eggs.

□ **Garden Nectar Plants:** perennial: lyre-leaf sage; biennial: thistles; annuals: Spanish needles, zinnias.

□ **Garden Host Plants:** perennial: wild sennas; annual: partridge pea.

□ **Identification:** 1.5 to 2.5 inches. A medium-sized sulphur with melon-orange above surrounded by variable dark umber brown or blackish margins. There is no eye spot on the underside of the hind wing while the butterfly is nectaring.

□ **Caterpillar:** The green caterpillar is covered by velvety short hairs that give it a unique sheen. There is a pale line down each side of the caterpillar.

□ **Chrysalis:** The green chrysalis looks like a

A Sleepy Orange nectaring.

Plant a patch of annual partridge pea or perennial sennas for Sleepy Oranges to lay their eggs on and raise a new generation. Plant or don't mow early-blooming lyre-leafed sage or late-blooming Spanish needles in the deep South, which provide important nectar sources for this butterfly. Throughout their range, single-type zinnias are a sure bet to lure Sleepy Oranges to nectar from midsummer to frost.

mini Cloudless Sulphur chrysalis with a long, pointed head and a flattened big belly—the color and shape helps it mimic a leaf to avoid predation.

▫ **Local Relative:** Tailed Orange (*Eurema proterpia*) is very similar but has no black margin on the hind wing, and winter forms have a pointed tail-like projection on their hind wings. It is an avid garden resident of south Texas and rarely strays into the Southwest or the southern Great Plains.

A Sleepy Orange pauses for a rest on rocks.

Dainty Sulphur

Nathalis iole

An old name of this butterfly is the "Dainty Dwarf," as it is one of the smallest butterflies. It is in the sulphur family so it is now more appropriately named. Dainty refers to its diminutive size, its delicate colorations and its habits.

But there are some attributes to this unique sulphur that are decidedly undainty. The Southwestern populations of this amazing little jewel, which is never more than 1¼ inches in size, regularly colonize areas as much as 1,000 miles to the north—including much of the Midwest. Following wet years, they may colonize Mediterranean California and stray throughout much of the West, except for the Pacific Northwest.

The peninsular Florida and southeast Georgia butterflies are from a different race and actually colonized themselves in their new permanent American range from the West Indies around 1913. Floridian and Georgian butterflies do not colonize northward like their southwestern cousins.

Summer butterflies of all Dainty Sulphurs are a bit more richly colored with traces of orange along the underside margin of their forewing. In late fall, the butterflies have a more dusty gray hue and may overwinter in the deep South but will not survive the winter in northern regions.

❑ **Status:** Dainty Sulphur is a resident in the Southwest and peninsular Florida where it overwinters as an adult butterfly. It is a regular colonist in the Midwest, western South and warm-summer regions of the West.

❑ **Habitat:** Dainty Sulphurs prefer flat, dry, open woods and savannas, roadsides, dunescapes, dry prairies and old fields.

❑ **Garden Habit:** Dainty Sulphur is most common in the garden in fall when it searches out late nectar sources. Dainty Sulphurs linger around their favorite nectar sources more so than do Little or Sleepy Sulphurs, which continually patrol for mates or host plants.

❑ **Garden Nectar Plants:** perennials: asters, single chrysanthemums; annual: Spanish Needles.

❑ **Garden Host Plants:** perennials: asters, sneezeweeds; annuals: Spanish needles, cosmos, marigolds.

❑ **Identification:** 1 to 1.25 inches. Our tiniest sulphur, Dainty Sulphurs are yellow with black-tipped forewings and black along the edge of where both the

A grayish fall form of Dainty Sulphur visits the last chrysanthemum of the season.

TIPS
TO ATTRACT

Maintain patches of Spanish needles in the deep South. In other regions, plant annual single dwarf marigolds or perennial heath asters as good-bet host and nectar plants. Plant late-blooming single chrysanthemums like the cultivar 'Sheffield Pink', which Dainty Sulphurs will visit for nectar even after hard freezes, when its daisy-like outer-ray petals (florets) have fallen.

forewing and hind wing meet. While resting, Dainty Sulphurs have three black spots near the forewing's lower edge. Summer butterflies are more colorful from this view and may have a melon-orange wash along the base of the forewing. Hind wings are pale yellow in summer and gray dusted in fall or winter.

□ **Caterpillar:** The tiny pale green caterpillar has plush tiny hairs and a darker green, brown or pinkish stripe down its back, which matches markings on its host plant.

□ **Chrysalis:** The green or yellow-green chrysalis is fairly uniform, with a rounded head, unlike the pointed head of other sulphurs.

A closeup of a Dainty Sulphur nectaring.

GOSSAMERS

Gossamer butterflies are aptly named, they are so light and delicate. Gossamer species include the tiny coppers, hairstreaks, blues, elfins and metalmarks. These diminutive butterflies have some of the most exquisite patterns and iridescent colors of any of our garden butterflies, and can be attracted to gardens in droves. Gossamers will sit still for a close look, but be sure to buy a pair of close-focusing binoculars or you'll miss out on some of their fine detail.

Gallery of Coppers

Coppers are richly colored with iridescent purple over orange or brilliant orange-red. A few are gray-brown with these highlights. Most display silvery white or gray when they rest with their wings closed—showing highlights of orange punctuated with black spots.

Coppers usually only open their wings when they're perched, either showing off or basking. They are very territorial and, when males encounter each other, will flutter together in battle. Coppers occasionally venture into gardens near their open habitat in the Northeast, Midwest, Rocky Mountains and Pacific Coast. The three coppers with the most extensive range and affinities toward gardens are described below.

❑ **Status:** Coppers are resident butterflies wherever they're found. They survive the winter as an egg or young caterpillar.

❑ **Habitat:** The coppers most likely found in your garden favor open habitats, from wet meadows to old fields, pastures and vacant lots. Twelve additional species in the West and far North are more restricted to wetlands, prairies, chaparral and other undisturbed habitats.

❑ **Garden Habit:** Coppers often appear out of nowhere to nectar on their favorite garden flowers. Their visits are usually brief but they leave a rich and lasting image of their beautiful colors and patterns.

❑ **Identification:** (See each description.)

❑ **Garden Nectar Plants:** shrubs: dewberries, buckwheats; perennials: yarrow, milkweeds, ox-eye daisy, longleaf bluets, mountain mints, buttercups, arrowheads; annual: gomphrena; weedy plants: dogbanes, red and white clovers.

❑ **Garden Host Plants:** weedy and wetland plants in the dock and knotweed family.

PURPLISH COPPER

Lycaena helloides (1.75 to 2 inches)

Purplish Copper has the most extensive range of any copper and is exquisitely detailed and aptly named for its open wings of black polka dots washed in iridescent purple. Females lack the purple hue and are extensively bright orange—both sexes have a rich orange zigzag band along the margin of their hind wings. When they nectar with their wings closed they show some warm orange on the forewing, fading to mauve. The hind wing is also mauve with a stitched zigzag line of orange along the wing margin. There are two broods of Purplish Coppers in the Great Lakes region and as many as nine broods per season in California.

BRONZE COPPER

Lycaena hyllus (1.5 to 2 inches)

Bronze Copper is expanding its range westward and southward in agricultural areas. With its orange forewing grading into silver along the outer margin, it's quite distinctive

A Bronze Copper nectaring in typical pose with its wings closed.

while it nectars on flowers in your garden. The hind wing is silver with an orange band along the margin and both wings are punctuated with black polka dots. If you're lucky enough to see a Bronze Copper with its wings open, the males are an unpunctuated beautiful wash of iridescent violet; females are pale orange with black spotting on the forewing and gray on the hind wing—both sexes have an orange band along the margin of the hind wing.

The appropriately-named Purplish Copper, basking with open wings.

AMERICAN COPPER

Lycaena phlaeas (1 to 1.25 inches)

American Coppers are tiny jewels of bright orange and rich gray. Their coloration and pattern resembles a female Bronze Copper but they're smaller and much more richly colored. Unlike most coppers, male and female American Coppers look pretty much the same. Caterpillars pupate into a loosely woven cocoon, unlike most butterflies. This copper is found across the northern hemisphere (Eurasia, North Africa), where it is called Small Copper on the other side of the pond. Enjoy these little jewels in your country-side gardens.

An American Copper perched with its wings outspread.

An American Copper nectars on butterfly milkweed.

Great Purple Hairstreak

Atlides halesus

If you have mistletoe gracing the branches of a shade tree in your yard or neighborhood, you could receive more than just a kiss during the holidays. Chances are good that your garden will be graced by one of the most beautiful and tropical-looking of all temperate butterflies.

Great Purple Hairstreak is one of the largest hairstreaks but, like the whole family, is still small when compared to all butterflies. The body and wing scales of this butterfly's upper side are grooved to reflect a shimmering blue. You will get a glimpse of this as the butterfly flies by, but it never really opens its wings unless it's in the deadly embrace of a crab spider or other flower-hiding predator. The hind wings have hair-like tails, which give the gossamer butterflies known as hairstreaks their common name.

Great Purple Hairstreaks avidly nectar from garden flowers so they will give you a great look at them as they drink. They nectar with their blue iridescent wings closed, but the side view of charcoal black—highlighted with white body spots, orange abdomen and touches of red, iridescent turquoise and green—is unmistakable.

Great Purple Hairstreaks rub their hind wings together as they perch—in fact, all hairstreaks do this. Why? A hungry bird is more likely to mistake the moving hind wings' hairs for the butterfly's antennaed head and bite the wrong

Mistletoe, a parasitic evergreen shrub found in trees, is the host plant of the Great Purple Hairstreak.

end of the butterfly. The hairstreak escapes with only losing a hair or two—its real antennae and body intact.

▫ **Status:** Great Purple Hairstreaks are resident butterflies that survive the winter as a chrysalis.

▫ **Habitat:** Great Purple Hairstreaks are found in woodlands, forests and wooded suburbs where their host plant, mistletoe, grows. Mistletoe is an evergreen shrub that is parasitic on various trees. It's the same plant that is cut for holiday decorations and yuletide romantic tradition.

▫ **Garden Habit:** Great Purple Hairstreaks, like all hairstreaks, often perch high in the trees. Their flight is fast and erratic—males often quibble in tornadic flights. Hairstreaks will descend into gardens to nectar on their favorite flowers.

▫ **Garden Nectar Plants:** small trees: devil's walkingstick, wild plums; shrub: summersweet clethra; perennials: bonesets, goldenrods; annual: Spanish needles.

▫ **Garden Host Plants:** evergreen parasitic shrub: mistletoes.

▫ **Identification:** 1.25 to 2 inches. Great Purple Hairstreaks are the

Side view of a Great Purple Hairstreak on mistletoe.

TIPS
TO ATTRACT

There are three broods of Great Purple Hairstreaks in much of the country. Plant early-blooming wild plum to attract the spring brood to nectar, summersweet clethra to draw in the summer brood, and devil's walkingstick to provide nectar to the fall brood! Also, don't forget to protect mistletoe in your trees. Arborists will often recommend its removal but it takes a severe infestation on a sick tree for this evergreen parasitic shrub to truly damage your trees.

only charcoal-colored hairstreak in most of the country—only the Atala in south Florida is similarly colored but lacks hairstreaks and is a bit more brilliantly marked.

□ **Caterpillar/Chrysalis:** Both the caterpillars and the chrysalises are out of sight high up in the mistletoe.

□ **Local Relatives:** There are many species of hairstreaks across the continent. Many are difficult to identify and others are local and quite spectacularly marked. Those most likely encountered are shown on the following pages.

A Great Purple Hairstreak perches on its host plant, mistletoe.

Gallery of Eastern Hardy Hairstreaks

There are many species of resident hairstreaks that overwinter as chrysalises in eastern North America. The following four species are the most often encountered in yards and gardens. Many more species are restricted to wild lands. It can be challenging to differentiate the hairstreaks—most have tails at the base of their hind wings (hairs) and a gray or brown base color marked with various spots with lines and bands of black, white, red-orange or blue (the streaks).

Hairstreaks fly fast and erratically but are very tame and approachable while they perch or nectar. They visit flowers mainly in late morning and late afternoon. Hairstreaks can fall into what butterfly watchers call "LBJs"—little brown jobs—with remarkable details upon close inspection. Buy a pair of close-focusing binoculars to really see their exquisite detail and minute splashes of brilliant color.

STRIPED HAIRSTREAK

Satyrium liparops (1 to 1.75 inches)

Striped Hairstreaks have paired bicolored stripes on their wings. The stripes are black on the inside and white on the outside of the pair of stripes. Striped hairstreaks inhabit the edges of nearly any woods in eastern North America. Their favorite nectar sources are shrubs: New Jersey tea, sumacs, meadowsweet, viburnums; perennials: milkweeds, daisies, goldenrods; biennial: Queen-Anne's lace; weedy plants: dogbanes, sweet clovers. Striped Hairstreaks caterpillars feed on a wide range of plants, from shrubby blueberries and wild azaleas to small trees, including wild cherries, plums, crabapples, hawthorns and related plants.

BANDED HAIRSTREAK

Satyrium calanus (1.25 to 1.5 inches)

Banded Hairstreaks have a more-or-less continuous, lumpy, bicolored band that jogs across the underside of both the forewing and hind wing. This band, after which the hairstreak is named, is dark toward the body and white toward the wing edge. There are a few additional short bands both inside and outside the main band. Banded Hairstreaks are found around or near oaks in city parks, oak-filled yards and native woodlands. They nectar on the same plants as Striped Hairstreaks. Banded Hairstreaks are never found far from their host plant, oaks.

A Striped Hairstreak perches on nectar-rich dogbane blossoms.

A Banded Hairstreak lands on a blooming spiderwort.

Tropical milkweed—when flowering, a good nectaring plant for hairstreaks.

CORAL HAIRSTREAK

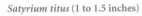

Satyrium titus (1 to 1.5 inches)

Coral Hairstreaks are one of the few hairstreaks without hairstreaks! Their tailless (hairless) hind wings are rimmed with a band of fiery coral-red spots. These brilliant spots

are just as distracting to a predator as are the hairstreaks on other species. Coral Hairstreaks' favorite nectar flowers include: shrubs: New Jersey tea, meadowsweet; perennials: milkweeds, coreopsis, longleaf bluets, mountain mints, black-eyed Susans; weedy plants: dogbanes, sweet clovers. Their caterpillars feed on wild cherries, wild plums and chokeberries.

JUNIPER HAIRSTREAK

Callophrys gryneus (1 to 1.25 inches)

Juniper Hairstreaks occur in both the East and West wherever junipers (often called redcedars in eastern North America) grow wild in abundance. In fact, a good way to find them is to shake or tap a juniper tree. Their olive coloration in the eastern part of their range is how they acquired their old common name, "Olive Hairstreak." Western Juniper Hairstreaks lack the green but still associate with junipers. Juniper Hairstreaks nectar on small trees: dogwoods, wild plums; shrub: dogwoods; perennials: yarrow, milkweeds; biennial: Queen-Anne's lace; annuals: shepherd's needles; weedy plants: dogbanes, winter cress, sweet clovers. Juniper Hairstreaks caterpillars feed solely on any species of juniper—the evergreen tree eastern redcedar being the most common species in the East.

A Coral Hairstreak on its favorite nectar source, butterfly milkweed.

A Juniper Hairstreak clutches onto a stem of its namesake host plant.

Gallery of Southeastern & Emigrant Hairstreaks

Of the many species of hairstreaks from the Southeast, three are common in gardens. The Gray Hairstreak regularly emigrates northward while the Red-Banded Hairstreak is mainly a resident. The third hairstreak, called the Atala, is limited to its Florida range but is an example of how gardeners have saved one of our most beautiful native butterflies.

GRAY HAIRSTREAK
Strymon melinus (1.25 to 1.5 inches)

Gray Hairstreaks are common across North America but are resident only in the South and Pacific West and colonize the rest of the country every summer. Gray Hairstreaks

A Gray Hairstreak basks on the leaf of a bloodflower milkweed.

are the most abundant hairstreaks in gardens, and their caterpillars can actually be pesky on certain plants like green beans. Their caterpillars eat an incredible array of plants, especially mallows like cotton, and legumes like beans and partridge pea. They nectar on many plants, including: shrub: butterfly bush; perennials: milkweeds, chrysanthemums, Joe-Pye-weed, bonesets, mountain mints, goldenrod; annual: globe amaranth.

RED-BANDED HAIRSTREAK
Calycopis cecrops (< 1 to 1.25 inches)

Red-Banded Hairstreaks have two hairs on each hind wing. The red band just inside the bicolored black-and-white

A Gray Hairstreak prepares to sip nectar from a lantana, one of its favorite nectar sources.

jagged line across the fore and hind wings is unmistakable. Red-Banded Hairstreaks are butterflies of the American Southeast but are expanding, colonizing or straying northward. They are one of the few butterflies that feed on dead, fallen leaves! The caterpillars feed in groups on the fallen leaves of sumacs, oaks and bayberries and, in Florida, on

A Red-Banded Hairstreak rubbing its hind wings, exposing the blue on the upper side of the opposite wing.

mango and manioc. You must provide a space for leaves to lie to have this butterfly, as its chrysalis is formed amidst the fallen dead leaves as well. Red-Banded Hairstreaks are common in gardens and will nectar on: tree: wild cherry; shrubs: New Jersey tea, summersweet clethra, sumacs; perennials: yarrow, milkweeds; annuals: Bidens and Spanish needles; weedy plant: dogbane.

ATALA HAIRSTREAK

Eumaeus atala florida (1.5 to 2 inches)

Though the Atala is found in only a small portion of the United States, it is one of our most strikingly colorful butterflies, and gardeners have saved it from the brink of extinction. Found only on the Florida Gold Coast and Keys, 30 years ago the butterfly was thought to be doomed by the rapid urbanization of the Miami-Fort Lauderdale-Palm Beach region. Gardeners have since planted wild coonties and other cycads, which are the Atala's only food plant, and the Atala adapted and has now prospered.

Atalas are limited in their northward spread because they cannot survive freezing weather, even though coonties and cycads are hardy into northern Florida. Atalas are black with phosphorescent aqua-blue bands of spots on their hind wing and body. A brilliant scarlet spot occurs on the hind wing adjacent to the butterfly's flaming orange abdomen. Male Atalas are iridescent green above and females are iridescent blue—but you'll never see a live butterfly with its wings open except in its slow and moth-like flight. Atalas are quite friendly and tame, and you can pick up and handle one without it streaking away like most other butterflies.

Atala caterpillars and chrysalises are colorful and readily observed, unlike the other hairstreaks'. They feed in groups and are bright pinky red with yellow spots. They also pupate in groups—the new chrysalises are covered with bitter droplets of sticky fluid. Atalas nectar on lantana and Spanish needles and can be abundant in gardens containing their host plants. Northern "snowbird" gardeners visiting or wintering on the Gold Coast are sure to encounter this gem.

An Atala Hairstreak, a stunning and beautiful butterfly of warm-weather areas.

Gallery of Western Hairstreaks

There are four resident hairstreaks that are quite widespread in the West and are apt to be found in gardens. Many, many species of hairstreaks inhabit the West but most are limited to more inaccessible habitats or are very localized. They may be brown, gray, green and even gold. Plant any wild buckwheat for a great nectar source for these "LBJs" (little brown jobs).

CALIFORNIA HAIRSTREAK

Satyrium californica (< 1 to 1.25 inches)

California Hairstreaks are brown-gray with rows of black dots on the outer part of both their fore and hind wings. The hind wing has a beautiful blue "eye" patch above the tail, which is capped and sided with orange. California Hairstreaks are butterflies of early summer and are found in hilly open oak woods, woodland edges and chaparral. California Hairstreaks visit a wide array of flowers and their host plants are oaks, buckbrush wild lilac and mountain mahogany.

A California Hairstreak nectaring on the blossoms of yarrow.

HEDGEROW HAIRSTREAK

Satyrium saepium (< 1 to 1.25 inches)

Hedgerow Hairstreaks are gray-brown with a jagged, stitched line across the fore and hind wings. The outer edge of the hind wing has V-shaped markings and an orangeless blue "eye" patch above the tail. The coppery-brown upper side of the wings is distinctive but seldom seen. Hedgerow Hairstreaks are also a butterfly of early summer and are found on edges of woodlands and chaparral. The butterfly's host plants are wild lilacs (especially buckbrush wild lilac) whose flowers the butterflies favor to nectar on as well. They also nectar on wild buckwheats and weedy plants like dogbanes.

The short, stubby hairstreaks help identify this Hedgerow Hairstreak.

THICKET HAIRSTREAK

Callophrys spinetorum (< 1 to 1.25 inches)

Thicket Hairstreaks are rich brown with a contrasting bicolored black (inner) and white (outer) band across their fore and hind wings. The upper side of the wings has a unique metallic blue wash. The tail is very short with an additional stub-like tail just above it. There are three blue patches above the tails—the middle patch or all three can be capped in orange. Thicket Hairstreaks are butterflies found high in coniferous trees where their host plant, the

The Gardener's Butterfly Book

parasitic dwarf mistletoe, grows on pines, firs and larches. They are common in late spring to late fall and have two broods, except in the northern part of their range where their only brood is present in early summer. They often come down from the treetops to puddle and sip nectar.

COLORADO HAIRSTREAK
Hypaurotis crysalus (1.25 inches)

Colorado Hairstreak is one of the most gorgeous of hairstreaks and the official state insect of Colorado. The upper side of the wings is iridescent purple with black outer edges and orange spots. The underside is pretty spiffy for a hairstreak—gray with black-and-white bands and outer spots of orange and blue. Its orange "eye" patch near the tail has a black "pupil." Colorado Hairstreaks are found in groves of Gambel oaks in Utah, Colorado, Arizona, New Mexico and bits of adjacent states. Gambel oak is the butterfly's host plant, and the butterfly nectars on sap from galls in the tree! They do not visit flowers to nectar. They are good reason to choose a Gambel oak for a shade tree, or carefully protect them on your property. Gambel oaks attract lots of other wildlife as well.

The crisp white band across rich brown wings identifies this Thicket Hairstreak, which is nectaring on wild onions.

A Colorado Hairstreak perches on its host plant, Gambel oak.

Eastern Tailed-Blue & Western Tailed-Blue

Everes comyntas and *Everes amyntula*

Eastern Tailed-Blue   Western Tailed-Blue

There are two species of tiny, tenacious butterflies with hair-like tails on their hind wings, just like the hairstreaks. They are in a group of butterflies called blues since most of the males of each species are beautiful hues of blue above. Tailed-Blues are silvery white underneath and the males are shimmering iridescent sky blue when they bask with their wings open in the morning sunlight. Females are mainly brown above.

The Eastern Tailed-Blue may be one of the most common butterflies over much of eastern North America (though it's found in places in the West too). The Western Tailed-Blue is its more wild western and northern counterpart. The two are very similar species, but the Western Tailed-Blue is usually larger and paler and has only one

A basking Western Tailed-Blue is nearly identical to its eastern counterpart.

orange spot by its tail, while Eastern Tailed-Blues have two or more. Most gardeners overlook this tiny jewel, which nectars on low flowers and loves to party at puddles. Eastern Tailed-Blues are found from early spring to late fall and are abundant in gardens while Western Tailed-Blues have only one late spring brood in the North and several broods in California.

◻ **Status:** Tailed-Blues are hardy, resident butterflies that survive the winter as a caterpillar that may hibernate in the fruit pod of its host plant.

◻ **Habitat:** Eastern Tailed-Blue is found in all sorts of open habitat, both native and human made. Western Tailed-Blue is more restricted to native open brushy habitats.

◻ **Garden Habit:** Tailed-Blues perform the same antic as hairstreaks and other blues—they rub their hind wings together while they bask, nectar and puddle. This gives predators the illusion that their moving tails are their real antennae and the hind wing spot(s) are their eyes—birds aim for this false head, and the butterfly usually escapes.

◻ **Identification:** Approximately 1 inch. The only blues on the continent with tails.

◻ **Garden Nectar Plants:** shrub: butterfly bush; perennials: milkweeds, asters, single chrysanthemums; annuals: Spanish needles, globe amaranth; weedy plants: clovers, dogbanes, fleabanes.

◻ **Garden Host Plants:** Eastern Tailed-Blues' caterpillars

A male Eastern Tailed-Blue basking.

Plant or protect white clover in your lawn for a large population of Eastern Tailed-Blues—clover is a favorite for them to nectar and raise a new brood on. Maintain a buffer area against your lawn, planted with vetches or milk vetches to attract the Western Tailed-Blue. Both these blues also like to sip moisture from puddles.

feed on the inflorescences (flower heads) and young fruit of many plants in the legume family: perennials: milk vetches, lupines, red clover, white clover and vetches. Western Tailed-Blues prefer to eat the fruit pods of the same or similar plants.

▫ **Caterpillar:** The tiny caterpillars are grub-like and easily overlooked.

▫ **Chrysalis:** The tiny chrysalis looks skull-like and is seldom seen.

A female Eastern Tailed-Blue is brown, with hints of bronze and green iridescence. This specimen is nectaring on bloodflower milkweed.

Spring Azure & Summer Azure

Celastrina ladon **and** *Celastrina neglecta*

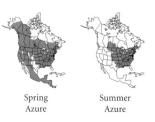

Spring
Azure

Summer
Azure

The world of these stunningly beautiful iridescent azure miniature butterflies is little understood by us intellectual life forms. From earliest spring to early fall a procession of these nearly identical butterflies emerges to lay eggs on the flower clusters of various shrubs and trees.

We have just recently noticed that the early spring butterflies are their own species—the Spring Azure—which is found across much of the continent and called "Echo Blue" in California. The later-emerging azures are now called Summer Azures and are limited in distribution to the eastern two-thirds of the continent. There may be as many as six different species in the East alone—but not to worry—four of them are quite limited in occurrence where their unique host plants grow.

Male Spring and Summer Azures are evenly blue above with no border. Female azures (both species) are blue, too, but have a dark forewing border, and female Summer Azures' lower wing is whitish. Spring Azure is among the earliest garden butterflies to emerge, and a welcome harbinger of the butterfly season. Summer Azures are a refreshing splash of cool blue on sultry summer days.

▫ **Status:** Azures are resident butterflies that overwinter as a chrysalis.

▫ **Habitat:** Azures are found in any habitat where their host plant trees and shrubs occur, so as a result are common in gardens.

▫ **Garden Habit:** Azures readily live their entire lives in your garden, provided you don't deadhead or trim off the flowers of their host trees and shrubs—the caterpillars feed among the flowers and forming fruit. Look for them nectaring and feeding on white clover in your lawn.

▫ **Identification:** <1 to 1.5 inches. With their wings closed they are tailless, silvery white and have various black dashes and flecks—not rounded spots.

▫ **Garden Nectar Plants:** shrubs: New Jersey tea and wild lilacs,

A Summer Azure nectars with its wings closed.

Plant several species of dogwoods with different bloom times to attract azures into your yard. Flowering dogwood and Pacific dogwood have beautiful showy white-bracted flowers in spring, while other small tree and shrub dogwoods have white masses of tiny flowers from spring into early summer, depending on the species. Plant California buckeye in the Pacific West to ensure a place for Spring Azures ("Echo Blues") there.

blackberries; perennial: milkweeds; weedy plants: dogbanes and clovers.

□ **Host Plants:** Azures' caterpillars feed on the inflorescences (flower clusters) of many trees and shrubs—Spring Azures feed on spring-flowering plants, and Summer Azures on summer-flowering plants. Shade tree: black cherry; small trees: California buckeye, flowering and Pacific dogwoods, toyon, coffeeberry; shrubs: New Jersey tea, dogwoods, wild cherries, sumacs and viburnums.

□ **Caterpillar/Chrysalis:** Both are similar to Tailed-Blues.

A Spring Azure is nearly identical to the Summer Azure but Spring Azures are more widespread, and some of the earliest butterflies to emerge in spring.

Gallery of Tropical Blues

Five species of blues found year-round in frost-free regions of the country emigrate northward in summer to colonize the Southwest, Midwest and/or deep South: a remarkable feat for such delicate, diminutive life forms.

Tropical Blues are frequent visitors to gardens and puddles—both males and females sip moisture. They are even tinier than the hairstreaks and show off a beautiful detailed coloration—another reason to buy that pair of close-focusing binoculars! Plant white clover and frogfruit in your lawn to encourage these gorgeous butterfly guests.

▫ **Status:** Tropical Blues are colonists or strays in much of the hottest parts of the continent, surviving the winter only in frost-free regions, where they are present all year.

▫ **Habitat:** These blues prefer open habitat, including woods, savannas, prairies, fields, deserts, coastal marshes, dunes and gardens.

▫ **Garden Habit:** Tropical blues are tiny and easily overlooked. They love to nectar and puddle (both males and females) and can be abundant in southwestern and southern gardens. Watch for them carefully in midwestern gardens in late summer—you will eventually spot one!

▫ **Garden Host Plants:** These blues' caterpillars mainly feed on the flowers, fruit and, occasionally, young leaves of: small trees: acacias, mesquite; shrubs: indigobush or feather dalea; perennials: prairie clovers and daleas, alfalfa; and many weedy legumes.

▫ **Caterpillar:** The tiny caterpillars of these blues are often tended by ants, which eat the caterpillar's sugary excretions and in turn protect the larvae from attack by other predators.

▫ **Chrysalis:** The Tropical Blue's chrysalis is teeny-tiny and seldom, if ever, observed.

WESTERN PYGMY BLUE

Brephidium exilis (0.5 to 0.75 inches)

Western Pygmy Blue is the world's smallest butterfly. They are so tiny that they are difficult to see in the garden. Western Pygmy Blues are easily identified, with their wings closed, by their tiny size, chestnut brown underside with white scaling and the row of metallic black spots at the base of the hind wing. Their host plants include non-legumes like saltbush and pigweed.

MARINE BLUE

Leptotes marina (1 inch)

Marine Blues were formerly called the "Striped Blue" for their white "zebra"-striped tan undersides. It's almost unbelievable that such tiny butterflies regularly emigrate from frost-free parts of the Southwest to colonize the entire

The Western Pygmy Blue is our tiniest butterfly.

A Marine Blue perched on its host plant, alfalfa.

Southwest and even parts of the Midwest as far north as Minnesota. This tiny blue is often overlooked, so be sure to take a close look at any late-season blue that visits alfalfa fields and gardens in the Southwest or Midwest.

CASSIUS BLUE

Leptotes cassius (0.75 to 1 inch)

Cassius Blue was formerly called the "Tropical Striped Blue." They are almost identical to the Marine Blue but their zebra-striped pattern looks tan-striped on white. They range from Southwest to Southeast and don't readily colonize the Midwest. They are the most common blue in Florida gardens. They nectar on frogfruit and Spanish needles; host plants include plumbagos and weedy pea family plants.

A Cassius Blue in its zebra stripes.

CERAUNUS BLUE

Hemiargus ceraunus (0.75 to 1 inch)

Ceraunus Blue was formerly called the "Southern Blue." They are silvery gray with white markings forming spots and bands. There is one (or two) strong marginal "eye" spot and a pair of black spots on the upper edge of the hind wing. Ceraunus Blues are common in open woods and deserts and in gardens near such habitats. Ceraunus Blues' favorite nectar plant is Spanish needles, in the Southeast, and beebush in the Southwest.

REAKIRT'S BLUE

Hemiargus isola (0.75 to 1 inch)

Reakirt's Blue was once called "Mexican Blue," as it's found year-round in Mexico but readily colonizes the Southwest and Great Plains-Midwest. Reakirt's Blues can be identified with their wings closed by their chain of large, round black spots on the forewing and black spots on the hind wing corner. Reakirt's Blues nectar on clovers and mints.

A Reakirt's Blue nectaring on the blossom of a long-headed coneflower.

A Ceraunus Blue perched amongst yellow composite blossoms.

Gallery of Spotted Blues

Spotted Blues can be identified by the distinct spots and patterns of spots on their wings. They are resident butterflies that overwinter as a chrysalis. The caterpillars are tended by ants, and adults puddle (both sexes) and sip nectar on a wide variety of low flowers. The western states are graced by many species that are difficult or impossible to differentiate (without experts dissecting them), and many are restricted to small remnants of native habitat. These are all hardy resident blues that overwinter as chrysalises. The following four species are those you are most likely to encounter.

ACMON BLUE

Icaricia acmon (0.75 to 1 inch)

Acmon Blue is the most common blue in the Pacific West at low elevations and will readily venture into your garden. Males are powdery blue above while females are brown (with a shot of blue, especially the early brood), and both have a pinkish orange band on their hind wing margin—called an aurora. The butterflies are variable and can be nearly identical to the Lupine Blue. Wild buckwheats are both the favored host plant and nectar plant, but Acmon Blues also feed and nectar on milk-vetches, silver lotus and clovers.

A female Acmon Blue nectars on a cinquefoil, and displays brown above.

A male Acmon Blue displays a blue upper side.

An Acmon Blue perches with its wings closed.

LUPINE BLUE

Icaricia lupini (1 inch)

Lupine Blue is the most ubiquitous western blue. Male Lupine Blues differ from Acmon Blues by having wide, dark margins. Both sexes have a spot in the middle of the forewing (called a cell spot) and black capping to their orange aurora, which Acmon Blue doesn't have. Lupine Blues favor mountainous and hilly areas over the lowlands favored by the Melissa Blue, described next. Lupine Blues' favorite nectar and host plant is once again the wild buck-wheat. In spite of its name, the Lupine Blue does not feed on lupines!

A Lupine Blue on a yellow composite flower.

MELISSA BLUE

Lycaeides melissa (< 1 to 1.25 inches)

Melissa Blue was once called the "Orange-Margined or Orange-Bordered Blue" because of its orange band on the underside of both the fore and hind wing margins. Melissa Blue is not named after a person; melissa means honey in Greek. Males are shimmering lavender blue above, while females are brown above with an orange marginal band on both wings. Melissa Blue's eastern subspecies, the Karner Blue, is restricted to sandy open woods where wild lupines, its host plant, grow—and is officially listed as threatened under the Endangered Species Act. Melissa Blues are abundant in meadows, prairies and fields in the intermountain West and Great Plains where they are the most common species of blue—these are the ones apt to visit your garden. Their host plants are wild licorice, various lupines and even alfalfa.

A Melissa Blue has a series of orange border spots on all of its wings and was once known as the Orange-Bordered Blue.

SILVERY BLUE

Glaucopsyche lygdamus (< 1 to 1.25 inches)

The Silvery Blue is a real gem of late spring—iridescent silvery blue above and brown-silver-gray below. A distinctive irregular row of round black spots, each with a white ring, line up across both the fore and hind wings. This blue has no marginal markings like the above three species. A subspecies of this butterfly is the only butterfly known to have become extinct in North America—the Xerces Blue was once found in western San Francisco. A victim of development, the last one was collected on March 23, 1943. (It is how the insect conservation organization, the Xerces Society, got its name.) Silvery Blues are widespread across the continent but prefer wild open habitat. They will venture into gardens adjacent to wild lands but signify the need to protect wild meadows, prairies and bogs. Silvery Blues nectar on late-spring plants in the aster family, and their host plants include: perennials: milk-vetches, lupines, alfalfa and vetches.

The appropriately named Silvery Blue is the most iridescent of all the blues.

Gallery of Elfins

When you need a butterfly fix after a long, cold winter, the first butterflies you should look for in spring are the elfins. Elfins are types of hairstreaks, but they lack the hind wing hairs and all have a more or less marbled-brown look to them—the quintessential "LBJs" (little brown jobs).

□ **Status:** Elfins are resident butterflies that overwinter on the ground beneath their host plants as a chrysalis. They visit puddles to imbibe moisture and visit early-season flowers for nectar.

□ **Local Relatives:** There are several similar species, most of which are found in northern or montane forests. Western Pine Elfin (*Callophrys eryphon*) is the western pine country counterpart to the Eastern Pine Elfin. Henry's Elfin (*Callophrys henrici*) can be a part of your garden if you live near wild eastern redbuds. To retain elfins in your garden, be sure to provide undisturbed mulched areas beneath host plants to protect overwintering chrysalises.

BROWN ELFIN

Callophrys angustinus (1 inch)

Brown Elfins are found in open barrens in the eastern mountains and across Canada through the mountainous West to the Pacific coast where they are found in chaparral.

They will readily venture into your garden if you are adjacent to these wild lands. Their host plants are all sorts of blueberries, huckleberries, bearberries and manzanitas in the heath family, and chaparral plants, including wild lilacs. The caterpillars feed on the flowers and developing fruits of their host plants.

The Eastern Pine Elfin emerges in spring even before the snow is gone.

EASTERN PINE ELFIN

Callophrys niphon (1.25 inches)

Eastern Pine Elfins are found in pine country from east Texas to New England across the Great Lakes into central Canada. Their Latin name, *niphon*, is Greek for snow—they often emerge before the last snows. They are always associated with their host plants—young stands of pines, including those you have planted in your yard. Eastern Pine Elfins nectar on early-blooming trees and shrubs, including spicebush, wild plums, willows and blueberries, but their favorite flower is a perennial—the early-blooming pussytoes. The late brood nectars on milkweeds and other weedy plants like dogbanes and fleabanes.

A Brown Elfin, out early, lands on winter-weathered foliage.

Gallery of Metalmarks

Metalmarks are a mainly tropical family of butterflies that are technically not in the Gossamer family of butterflies. Metalmarks got their name from the markings on their wings, which look just like shiny bits of metal. Male metalmarks usually rest upside down under a leaf and watch for passing mates. They puddle to imbibe moisture, and drink nectar from buckwheat and aster family flowers.

Even the experts are stumped to define all the metalmark species found in the Southwest, so don't worry about which species you encounter—just enjoy their unique beauty. Most metalmarks are quite habitat restricted, so they seldom visit gardens except for ones at the edge of their domain.

◻ **Status:** Metalmarks are resident butterflies that overwinter as a chrysalis.

◻ **Garden Nectar Plants:** shrubs: seepwillow and wild buckwheats; perennials: mainly composites like yarrow, ox-eye daisy, coreopsis, sneezeweeds, black-eyed Susans and goldenrods.

◻ **Garden Host Plants:** thistles and ragwort (East), wild buckwheats, seepwillow and mesquites (West).

◻ **Caterpillar:** The tiny caterpillars are slug-like and covered with dense tufts of hairs.

MORMON METALMARK

Apodemia mormo (0.75 to 1.25 inches)

Mormon Metalmark is the predominant metalmark of the 15 western species—found throughout much of the Southwest and sparingly northward into Canada. Along the Mexican border from California through Texas, the Fatal Metalmark (*Calephelis nemesis*) is the easiest to entice into

gardens, as it favors disturbed habitat. You will certainly have it in your garden if you plant its host and nectar source shrub—the seepwillow. In the Sonoran and western Chihuahaun Zones the Palmer's Metalmark (*Apodemia palmeri*) is easily attracted into gardens where its food plant tree, honey mesquite, grows. Three species reside in the East: Little Metalmark (*Calephelis virginiensis*), Northern Metalmark (*Calephelis borealis*) and Swamp Metalmark (*Calephelis mutica*). Little Metalmark is the most easily encountered in pine flatwoods of the Southeast.

The Blue Metalmark is one of many western species and the easiest metalmark to identify because of its blue coloration.

This Fatal Metalmark shows off the typical metal-looking marks that give these butterflies their name.

Mormon Metalmark—most common metalmark of the West.

BRUSHFOOTS

*T*he brushfoots define the largest butterfly family in North America. They are called brushfoots because their brush-like first pair of front legs are atrophied and cannot be used for walking or perching. The brushfoot butterflies are primarily orange and brown but a few are black, white and blue as well. They exhibit a wide array of patterns, shapes and life histories, and several species are sure to inhabit every garden.

American Snout

Libytheana carinenta

American Snout is the Jimmy Durante of butterflies, but its long "snout" is not a nose or a beak—it's actually the two protective proboscis (tongue) coverings called palpi. No other North American butterfly has such elongated palpi. The reason for this long snout is probably to aid in camouflage. Snout butterflies look like dead leaves and petiole (leaf stalk)—it's their long snout that mimics the petiole. The butterflies hold their antennae forward in line with their snout as well. The female American Snout is also unusual because all six of her legs are working legs. It does not have the atrophied first pair of legs characteristic of the brushfoot butterflies. American

An American Snout in typical pose showing its long "snout" and antennae which it holds forward.

Snout can have periodic population explosions—especially in the Rio Grande Valley—when thousands of butterflies may be in flight.

□ **Status:** American Snouts are resident in mild-winter regions and regular to irregular colonists at the north edge of its range.

□ **Habitat:** American Snout prefers floodplain areas where its host plants, sugarberries and hackberries, are most abundant and mud for puddling is prevalent. Sugarberries and hackberries have spread into hedgerows and other woodlands and brushlands, so the American Snout may show up almost anywhere.

□ **Garden Habit:** American Snouts are not regular nectarers but can't resist globe amaranth flowers and butterfly feeders filled with overripe fruit. They seem to appear from thin air because of their fast erratic flight. They act skittish but can become very tame and land on you to imbibe salt off your skin.

Another American Snout—an understated but still subtly beautiful butterfly.

Plant a hackberry or sugarberry tree as a shade tree—both are great substitutes for elms, and are host plants for American Snouts. In small spaces and in the Southwest, the netleaf hackberry is a good substitute. Plant globe amaranths for American Snouts to nectar on. Install a butterfly feeder filled with overripe fruit.

□ **Garden Nectar Plants:** small trees: woolly bumelia, wild plums, peach; shrubs: summersweet clethra, dogwoods, rabbitbrush, seepwillow; perennials: asters, goldenrods; annuals: lantana, globe amaranth; weedy plant: dogbane.

□ **Garden Host Plants:** shade tree: hackberry, sugarberry; small trees: Lindheimer hackberry, netleaf hackberry; shrubs: dwarf hackberry, spiny hackberry.

□ **Identification:** 1.5 to 2 inches. American Snout is easily identified by its long "snout" (described above). No other butterfly has this readily seen field mark.

□ **Caterpillar:** The caterpillar is seldom seen but is green with tiny yellow spotting and three yellow racing stripes—one on each side and one down its back.

□ **Chrysalis:** The green chrysalis is marked with a horizontal yellow line that resembles a leaf's midvein—this makes the chrysalis look more leaf-like and thus unseen by hungry predators.

An American Snout nectaring on mistflower with its wings outspread. This is a rare scene; snouts usually nectar with their wings closed!

Zebra
Heliconius charithonius

The life history of the Zebra is remarkable. They are unique in what they eat—pollen. What's so special about eating pollen? It's rich in proteins and amino acids that help the Zebra live longer. Nectar is just sugar water and provides only energy to burn (Zebras do eat some nectar though).

Zebras easily live six months in the wild with no hibernation and they can remember where the best flowers are. Their host plants are passionvines, which the Zebra caterpillars ingest, utilizing the plant's toxins to become poisonous themselves. The passionvines fight back by producing egg-like growths to discourage Zebras from laying eggs on them! A whole subfamily of American tropical (neotropical) butterflies feed on passionvines and do this—all are poisonous and have characteristically long forewings. They are collectively called "longwings" or Heliconians by scientists, and the Zebra is often appropriately known as the "Zebra Longwing."

Snowbirds spending the winter in Florida or south Texas, or families who visit Disney World, are sure to encounter this butterfly. It also lives well in captivity and can be observed at butterfly houses across the country.

□ **Status:** Zebras are a resident butterfly that flies year-round. They are a rare stray northward—especially in the southern Great Plains.

□ **Habitat:** Zebras inhabit tropical hammocks, semitropical woodlands and wooded gardens containing their host and nectar plants.

□ **Garden Habit:** Zebras have a slow, almost wobbly flight and routinely nectar from flowers throughout the garden

The white caterpillar of the Zebra is toxic and feeds on various passionvines.

The Julia is a relative of the Zebra but has velvety orange wings.

and neighborhood just as a bee would. This behavior is called trap-lining. They roost together in a sheltered small tree and emit an odor to deter predators.

□ **Garden Nectar Plants:** shrubs: firebush, ixoras, lantana; vines: tropical cucumber, Mexican flame vine; perennial: pentas; annual: shepherd's needles. All these plants are annual in areas with freezing winters.

□ **Garden Host Plants:** perennial vines: native and hybrid passionvines (see Gulf Fritillary).

□ **Identification:** 2.75 to 4 inches. Zebras have exceptionally long wings that are chocolate brown with yellow stripes—no other butterfly is shaped or patterned this way. Zebras are poorly named, as they are not black and white—their old name, "Yellow-Barred Heliconian," was most descriptive.

□ **Caterpillar:** Zebra caterpillars are white with barbed black spines.

T I P S
TO ATTRACT

Plant passionvines to allow the butterflies to colonize. A large live oak is a great shelter against light winter frosts. Plant a warm-colored border of cream, gold and orange varieties of lantana with scarlet flowering firebush intermingled—the back of the border could be a trellis of showy Mexican flame vine with the less showy but pollen-rich tropical cucumber intertwined.

◻ **Chrysalis:** The golden brown chrysalis is irregularly shaped with two antler-like horns on its head. Upon close inspection from the back, the antlers become two jaws on a fierce-looking creature—but, overall, the caterpillar looks like a dried, crinkled leaf.

◻ **Local Relative:** Julia (*Dryas julia*) is a fast-flying long-winged cousin of the Zebra with bright orange wings and a similar host preference of passionvines; especially many-flowered and corky-stemmed passionvines. Julias are found together with Zebras and don't range as far north in Florida but they stray northward in the Great Plains as well. Julias do well in captivity just like the Zebra and can be seen in most butterfly houses across the country.

A Zebra sipping nectars from a Mexican sunflower.

Gulf Fritillary

Agraulis vanillae

ulf Fritillary is truly a "WOW" butterfly—their brilliant red-orange upper side and underside painted with silvery metallic brush-stroke-like spots make them a sight to behold. The butterfly is well named, as it is most common near the Gulf of Mexico, but it is also prevalent in the Southwest and is introduced in Hawaii.

This butterfly likes it hot! Many books show it ranging into the upper Midwest, but this is a misnomer. A Gulf Fritillary in the North is truly a rare event indeed and cause for celebration if you're lucky enough to host one in your northern butterfly garden. (I haven't seen one in the upper Midwest for 30 years—since I was a child—but I remember it well.)

Gulf Fritillaries are actually closer relatives to the Zebra than to the fritillaries. Their wings are elongated like other longwing butterflies, and their host plants are passionvines, so they are poisonous as well. Gulf Fritillaries often nectar with the giant yellow Cloudless Sulphur, both of which have continuous emergence and no synchronized hatches like the cyclical-brooded swallowtails. Their continual garden presence and brilliant colors make them the quintessential garden butterflies of the South.

▫ **Status:** Gulf Fritillaries are resident only in frost-free or nearly frost-free locations where they survive the winter as a chrysalis. They are a colonist in much of the South and Southwest and a stray northward.

▫ **Habitat:** Gulf Fritillaries frequent open woods and disturbed habitat. They congregate in yards and gardens that contain their favorite nectar sources.

▫ **Garden Habit:** A showy and welcome butterfly that may live its entire life in the garden. Gulf Fritillaries open and close their wings while they nectar—showing off their brilliant orange upper side and stunning, shining silver-spotted underside. They are toxic to birds, so are pretty pugnacious. If you provide their host plant, native passionvines, they will colonize your garden and you will have a continuous hatch of butterflies until frost.

▫ **Garden Nectar Plants:** perennial: *Verbena bonariensis*; annuals: Spanish needles, annual vinca, lantana, Mexican sunflower, zinnias.

▫ **Garden Host Plants:** perennial vines: passionvines, mainly the native and native hybrid species, including maypop, yellow passionflower, corky-stemmed passionflower and the gorgeous hybrid passionvine cultivar called 'Incense'.

The fabulous brushstokes of metallic silver on the underside of the Gulf Fritillary make it one of our most beautiful butterflies.

□ **Identification:** 3 to 3.75 inches. Gulf Fritillaries are long-winged and brilliant red-orange above; their undersides shine with the most metallic-silver elongated spotting of any butterfly.

□ **Caterpillar:** The red-orange and black striped caterpillar has black spines from head to end—typical warning coloration for a toxic caterpillar.

□ **Chrysalis:** The jagged chrysalis hides by looking like a dead leaf.

A Gulf Fritillary perches, with wings outspread, on a gazania blossom.

Variegated Fritillary

Euptoieta claudia

Variegated Fritillaries are not really that variegated in color, they're just a range of orange hues. Irregular lines of black define a tawny, almost cinnamon, orange area close to the body, a mid-wing band-like patch of pale creamy orange, and wing margins of lighter tawny orange containing a series of black spots.

This butterfly is the "middle child" of the fritillaries and fits somewhere between the more brilliant Gulf Fritillary and the stunning Greater or "true" fritillaries. It doesn't have the long wings of the Gulf Fritillary but has more elongated wings than the Greater Fritillaries. It lacks the silver spangles on the underside of the hind wing that other fritillaries have, but shares host plants from both fritillary groups (it eats both violets and passionvines).

It is the friendliest of the fritillaries, and individuals will readily take up residence in your garden. Variegated Fritillaries show up in gardens in spring when the white clover begins to bloom, and if you have their host plants for new broods to emerge, you will have Variegated Fritillaries all summer until frost. Most of your butterflies will move on—colonizing new areas to the north.

◻ **Status:** Variegated Fritillary is a resident butterfly that flies all year in frost-free regions and overwinters as a chrysalis in much of the mild-winter parts of the country. The butterfly annually colonizes much of the remaining warm-summer regions of the continent.

◻ **Habitat:** Open woods and grassy meadows and other disturbed habitat, including yards and gardens.

◻ **Garden Habit:** Variegated Fritillaries take up residence if your garden is flower filled and their host plants—passionvines or violets—are present. You will recognize some individual butterflies that set up territories in parts of your garden on their favorite flowers, and notice how their colors dramatically fade over time from bright orange when newly born to pale creamy orange when they're a couple of weeks old.

◻ **Garden Nectar Plants:** perennials: milkweeds, asters; annuals: Spanish needles, bur marigolds, sulphur cosmos, marigolds; weedy plants: mustards, dogbanes and clovers.

◻ **Garden Host Plants:** perennial vine: passionvines; perennial: violets; annuals: wild flaxes, pansies, violas.

A Variegated Fritillary feeds on the nectar-rich blossoms of a butterfly bush.

Variegated Fritillaries can be encouraged to reside in your garden if you plant pansies or violas for spring color, then let single marigolds or sulphur cosmos overtake them in the summer heat. Allow your lawn to contain white clover and violets, or at least have a patch of violets in a shaded bed. Plant a passionvine for an additional host plant.

Identification: 1.75 to 3.25 inches. Variegated Fritillaries are medium-sized with relatively long wings—rich orange above but fading to tawny golden orange as they age. They are roughly marbled below without any striking markings as with other fritillaries.

Caterpillar: The colorful caterpillar is orange-red and white striped with 12 rows of branched spines—the front two spines point forward over their head.

Chrysalis: The chrysalis may be stunningly beautiful—white studded in orangy gold—but does not look very appetizing.

A Variegated Fritillary basks with its wings open to catch the sun's warming rays.

Great Spangled Fritillary

Speyeria cybele

The Great Spangled Fritillary's name says it all—even the Latin name *cybele* is after Cybele—the mythical Greek and Roman nature goddess—great mother of all gods. Great Spangled Fritillary is a medium- to large-sized butterfly and nearly the largest of its clan, known as the greater fritillaries (only the Diana and Regal Fritillary in the following gallery, page 134, can be larger). The underside hind wing is spangled with metallic silver spots, which gleam in the sunshine.

Great Spangled Fritillaries have only one brood of butterflies per season but are in flight throughout the summer. Males emerge first and then females at midsummer. Females lay a lot of eggs, for a butterfly—more than 1,000 and some even more than 2,000—but they seem to lay them willy-nilly—not on their host plant of violets. The tiny, newly emerged caterpillar hibernates through the winter, then finds violets to feed on when springtime returns.

❑ **Status:** A hardy resident butterfly that survives the winter as a new caterpillar. Great Spangled Fritillaries are declining in numbers in the West.

❑ **Habitat:** Great Spangled Fritillaries inhabit open woods and woodland edges, marshes, meadows and prairies and other disturbed habitat with violets present. They visit yards and gardens near wild areas with violets and have proved to be the most adaptable of the Greater Fritillaries in most of their range.

❑ **Garden Habit:** Great Spangled Fritillaries visit gardens to nectar on their favorite flowers. Groups of Great Spangled Fritillaries will often congregate and nectar together on their favorite flowers. They alight with open wings and conduct shallow, slow, pulsing wing beats while they sip nectar from the flowers. They seldom visit long, unless you can host them with an unmaintained area where groundcover is interspersed with violets.

❑ **Garden Nectar Plants:** perennials: milkweeds, purple coneflowers, Joe-Pye-weed, bergamots, ironweeds; biennial: thistles; annu-

The silvery spots on the underside of the Great Spangled Fritillary give this butterfly its name.

Plant a native perennial border of early summer-blooming stiff coreopsis and pale purple coneflowers, midsummer-blooming purple coneflowers mixed with butterflyweed and late-summer-blooming swamp milkweed mixed with tall Joe-Pye-weeds at the back of the grouping. If you allow a place for non-invasive native thistles, Great Spangled Fritillaries are sure to oblige en masse. Native thistles generally have leaves with felty white undersides; the noxious-pest exotic thistles, like nodding thistle, bull thistle and Canada thistle (actually all Eurasian natives) do not. If you don't have a lot of space, then plant a patch of purple coneflowers—these fritillaries like the cultivar 'Magnus' just fine—it was voted a recent Perennial Plant of the Year.

al: *Verbena bonariensis*; weedy plant: dogbanes.

□ **Garden Host Plants:** perennials: violets, except for the European sweet violet, which kills the caterpillars.

□ **Identification:** 3 to 4 inches. Great Spangled Fritillaries are medium to large butterflies with a rich orange upper side being more cinnamon at the base of their wings. The underside hind wing is spangled with metallic silvery white spots and there is a wide creamy band before the hind wing margin's spots.

□ **Caterpillar:** The velvety black caterpillar with reddish or yellowish based spines is nocturnal and seldom seen.

□ **Chrysalis:** The chrysalis is dark mottled brown with a brown abdomen and is seldom encountered.

□ **Local Relatives:** See Gallery of Greater Fritillaries.

Great Spangled Fritillaries occasionally rest with their wings open.

Gallery of Greater Fritillaries

Most of the Greater Fritillaries have not adapted well to humans' changing of the land. Many are declining, representing the sad state of our modern environment and our lack of understanding in protecting wild areas—we either mismanage them or, just as bad, don't manage them at all. Though most of these fritillaries will never visit your garden, they are some of the most spectacular North American butterflies. Hopefully, they will inspire you to become involved in protecting and managing natural landscapes beyond your own property, yard or garden. Look for these when you are recreating in nature's glorious gardens.

DIANA

Speyeria diana (3.5 to 4.5 inches)

Dianas inhabit open forests and woodlands mixed with flowery meadows, glades or barrens—they are considered one of the continent's most beautiful butterflies, yet have disappeared from much of their range. Visit them in July at the annual Mount Magazine butterfly festival outside Paris, Arkansas.

A female Diana Fritillary.

REGAL FRITILLARY

Speyeria idalia (3.25 to 4.25 inches)

Regal Fritillary requires large expanses of carefully managed wild grasslands or native hay meadows. Regal Fritillaries have recently disappeared right before our conservationist eyes from most of the country between the Mississippi River and the Atlantic Coast!

Regal Fritillary is a butterfly of the prairies. This butterfly has nearly disappeared east of the Mississippi River.

NOKOMIS FRITILLARY

Speyeria nokomis (2.5 to 3.25 inches)

Nokomis Fritillary is losing the war for western water: it requires seeps and springs and accompanying wet meadows and marshes for a place to live.

Nokomis Fritillary is found in mountain seeps and wetlands.

CALLIPPE FRITILLARY
Speyeria callippe (2 to 2.5 inches)

A Callippe Fritillary nectaring on wild thistles.

MORMON FRITILLARY
Speyeria mormonia (1.5 to 2 inches)

A Mormon Fritillary nectaring on Gaillardia.

HYDASPE FRITILLARY
Speyeria hydaspe (1.5 to 2.25 inches)

A Hydaspe Fritillary on wild asters.

APHRODITE FRITILLARY
Speyeria aphrodite (3 to 3.5 inches)

An Aphrodite Fritillary taking nectar from dogbane.

Meadow Fritillary

Boloria bellona

Meadow Fritillaries are butterflies of cool, moist meadows, hayfields and pastures. Their Latin name, *bellona*—after the mythical Roman goddess of war who was Mars's sister—is difficult to understand, but most likely refers to their orange-red coloration.

Meadow Fritillaries have a peaceable nature about them as they peruse the meadows on long glider wings in search of romance. They nectar from any yellow daisy-related flower. Their meadow name is most appropriate because of their habitat needs, and they are definitely country folk that don't stray into the city unless there's an open grassy environment inviting them to do so. You can expect them in your garden only if you live near their meadowy or agricultural environs, and there they can be relatively common.

Meadow Fritillaries are expanding their range southward in some areas (Missouri and Kentucky) where agricultural hayfields and pastures have created additional living quarters for them. They are the most common and widespread of a group of similar fritillaries known as the lesser fritillaries—most of which are small with elongated wings— and reside in special habitats, mostly in the far North, alpine and tundra regions.

◻ **Status:** Meadow Fritillaries are a resident butterfly that overwinters as a caterpillar.

◻ **Habitat:** Meadow Fritillaries inhabit meadows. They are also found in disturbed grasslands, including roadsides to hayfields, pastures and pristine prairies, too.

◻ **Garden Habit:** Meadow Fritillaries are on constant patrol for females and fly low over the ground. If your yard is meadowy or full of rich plantings of flowers and grasses, then they may peruse your garden and visit and nectar for a bit. They seldom stray far away from grassy areas, so you won't encounter them in gardens in dense urban areas without open space nearby.

◻ **Garden Nectar Plants:** shrub: wild lilacs; perennials: ox-eye daisy, wild buckwheats, hawkweeds, forget-me-nots, black-eyed

The marbled underside of the Meadow Fritillary looks like a fallen dead leaf while it rests in the grass.

Identification: 1.5 to 2 inches. Meadow Fritillaries are medium-small butterflies with elongated wings. They are orange above with black spots and markings. They are more orange-brown below with marblings of rosy purples on the hind wing.

Caterpillar: The caterpillars are purplish black with brown spines and feed at night, but are rarely seen.

Chrysalis: The chrysalis is rarely seen but is brown with yellow mottling and highlights and gold cone-like bumps on its back.

Local Relative: Pacific Fritillary (*B. epithore*) (nearly identical) is the counterpart butterfly found in the Pacific Northwest and northern Rocky Mountains. Many similar species occur in the far North and high elevations—including alpine habitats unsuitable for most butterflies.

Susans, ragworts, vervains; annual: *Verbena bonariensis*; weedy plants: dogbanes and dandelion.

Garden Host Plant: perennial: violets.

The upper side of the beautiful Meadow Fritillary.

Silvery Checkerspot

Chlosyne nycteis

The Silvery Checkerspot is probably the lightest colored on its undersides of all the checkerspots, but is really not that silvery. Its Latin name is from another myth, as the species is named after the legendary Greek, Nykteus—the King of Thebes. Its Latin genus means "with the light green of spring," presumably because of its springtime emergence.

This is the most common checkerspot and found throughout much of the eastern two-thirds of the continent minus the coastal plain east of the Mississippi. The Silvery Checkerspot can be readily recognized by its slow,

A Bordered Patch nectars on wild mistflowers in Texas.

gliding flight along pathways and edge habitats. They perch and nectar—often on large daisy-like flowers, where they become the centerpiece.

In the North, there is one midsummer brood, but in the middle and southern part of its range there are two broods—one in early summer and one in late summer (there may be three broods in the deep South). They are similar to the crescents but are usually larger and aren't quite as ubiquitous in both habitat and presence through the whole growing season.

❑ **Status:** Silvery Checkerspots are a resident butterfly that overwinters as a partially grown caterpillar in a special brown skin—a sleeping bag, so to speak.

❑ **Habitat:** Silvery Checkerspots reside in woodlands, savannas, prairies, meadows and old fields. They reside in human-made landscapes, as long as they are not immaculately maintained, including: inner-city parks, yards and gardens near open spaces or in large yards that contain unmaintained spaces and exuberant flower borders.

❑ **Garden Habit:** Silvery Checkerspots make their favorite flowers come alive. They nectar from the centers of many species of daisy-like flowers, where they seem to become part of the flower. While they nectar they slowly raise and lower their wings as if thoroughly enjoying their meal. They chase each other or fly with long glides along flower border edges and paths through the garden.

❑ **Garden Nectar Plants:** perennials: milkweeds, all species of purple coneflowers, black-eyed Susans; annuals: marigolds, zinnias; weedy plants: clovers and dogbanes.

❑ **Garden Host Plants:** perennials: wingstem, asters, wild sunflowers, black-eyed Susans, crownbeards.

The underside of a Silvery Checkerspot while it rests on a tropical sage.

138

□ **Identification:** 1.5 to 2 inches. Silvery Checkerspots are on the large size of tiny—you could say they're small butterflies with a checkery-spotted pattern of blacks and oranges and a fringe of black and white. They are larger than the similar crescent butterflies.

□ **Caterpillar:** The tiny caterpillars feed in a herd and skeletonize a leaf (eating everything but the tough veins) before moving to the next. They are more or less black with black spines.

□ **Chrysalis:** The variably colored tiny chrysalis is seldom seen and in some places is formed under rocks.

□ **Local Relative:** Bordered Patch (*Chlosyne lacinia*) is the most widespread of a group of semitropical close relatives and is common in southwestern gardens. It rarely strays northward up the Great Plains as far as Kansas City in late summer and fall. It is easily identified by its cream, yellow or orange band-like patch, which stretches around the middle of each wing.

A Silvery Checkerspot nectars on black-eyed Susans.

Pearl Crescent

Phyciodes tharos

Pearl Crescents get their name from the pearly, crescent-shaped mark in the middle of the edge of the hind wing's underside. You will need your close-focusing binoculars to see it—and it is really only prevalent on female butterflies.

Pearl Crescents are common and abundant butterflies, with continuous broods throughout the entire growing season. You will find them in your roadside gardens and other disturbed edge habitats.

Pearl Crescents appear to be fun loving—always investigating each other and other butterflies—but this behavior is actually the males continuously looking for opportunities to check out the females. They congregate at puddles to drink moisture.

This butterfly has certainly benefited from our presence on the landscape and has increased in numbers as new disturbed edge habitat has been created. It is not found in the forest or dense tallgrass prairie.

▢ **Status:** Most crescents are resident butterflies overwintering as a caterpillar. Phaon and Texan Crescents are resident butterflies that are present year-round in frost-free regions and are regular colonists and strays northward.

▢ **Habitat:** Pearl Crescents inhabit any disturbed open habitat, including yards and gardens, but are especially abundant on roadsides, old fields and abandoned properties.

▢ **Garden Habit:** These tiny butterflies glide between their favorite flowers and spend time nectaring on many daisy-like (composite) flowers. They strongly pulse their open wings and slowly turn their bodies in a circular pattern that corresponds with their nectaring of the individual florets spiraled around the center of a composite's flower. Their

A Pearl Crescent shows its namesake pearly-colored, crescent-shaped mark at the back of its hind wing.

A Texan Crescent sips moisture caught between gravel.

nectaring behavior often draws attention to them when they would otherwise go unnoticed.

▢ **Garden Nectar Plants:** perennials: milkweeds, asters, black-eyed Susans; annuals: Spanish needles, Mexican zinnia; weedy plants: winter cress, clovers, fleabanes and dogbanes.

▢ **Garden Host Plants:** perennials: asters, wild buckwheat, frogfruit, and gumweed.

▢ **Identification:** 1.25 to 1.5 inches. A common tiny orange butterfly that rests with its wings open. The orange open wings are bordered in black with various scribbles and spots of black. The underside is creamy with some orange on the forewing—both wings have various brown marblings and scaling. Consult your field guide in the far North and western high country for Tawny Crescent (*Phy-*

Pearl Crescents readily nectar on a recent Perennial Plant of the Year—'Goldsturm' black-eyed Susan. Plant several species and varieties of black-eyed Susans (*Rudbeckias*) which bloom from early summer into fall and provide a continuous nectar source for crescents' many broods. Late-blooming asters and single chrysanthemums are a must for those butterflies searching for nectar in Indian summer (late fall after a frost) and will provide nectar for the wandering emigrant Phaon Crescent and Texan Crescent.

ciodes batesii) and Northern Crescent (*Phyciodes selenis*); in the deep South and Southwest for Phaon Crescent (*Phyciodes phaon*) and Texan Crescent; or in the West for Mylitta Crescent and Field Crescent (*Phyciodes pratensis*) to differentiate Pearl Crescent from these less widespread species—some of which cannot be accurately differentiated from Pearl Crescent outside of the lab!

▫ **Caterpillar:** The tiny black caterpillars have white side stripes and crosswise rows of branched spines—they are tiny and seldom noticed by gardeners.

▫ **Chrysalis:** The tiny, dark chrysalis is almost never encountered.

▫ **Local Relatives:** There are many very similar species, and those previously listed are those you are most likely to encounter.

A Pearl Crescent nectars on the tall blossoms of an ironweed.

Baltimore Checkerspot

Euphydryas phaeton

Baltimore Checkerspot is the state butterfly of Maryland, whose largest city shares its name. The black butterfly's spectacular pattern, with pale yellow and red-orange colored spots, warns would-be predators that "I'm poisonous." This butterfly, along with its red-and-black caterpillars and its related western cousins, are all poisonous to birds and mammals that try to eat them.

Baltimore Checkerspots emerge once a year and are found from late spring into mid-summer. They will fly from wetlands that grow their host plant, turtle-head,

and visit neighboring yards and gardens, where they nectar on such delicacies as butterflyweed and oddities like the rubber-band-smelling flower of the Japanese tree lilac. Recent laws protecting wetlands have really helped save a lot of this butterfly's habitat. Major residential developments now surround Baltimore Checkerspot filled wetlands in places like the suburbs of Minnesota's Twin Cities; not that long ago, the wetlands would have been drained and developed, but now gardeners in these subdivisions can enjoy Baltimores in their gardens. The more southerly forms of the butterfly do not inhabit wetlands, so will only visit gardens in open woods where natural grassy openings provide habitat.

□ **Status:** Baltimore Checkerspot is a resident butterfly that overwinters as a caterpillar sheltered in the fallen leaf litter.

□ **Habitat:** Most northern populations are associated with wetlands where their host plant, turtlehead, grows. Southerly populations are found in open woods, savannas and glades where their other host plant, false foxgloves, grows.

□ **Garden Habit:** Baltimores are rare visitors to the garden unless you are adjacent to their habitat. They visit to nectar on a select few plants, namely butterflyweed.

□ **Garden Nectar Plants:** Baltimore Checkerspots prefer overripe fruit and dung or smelly flowers like: small tree: Japanese tree lilac; shrub: viburnums; perennials: milkweeds, mountain mints; biennial: thistles; weedy plant: knapweed (a noxious carcinogenic plant you shouldn't grow).

□ **Garden Host Plants:** eggs are laid on perennials: turtlehead, penstemons and weedy English plantain (and non-cultivatable plants like false foxgloves); after overwintering, they may feed on a variety of plants, including shrubs and trees.

□ **Identification:** 1.75 to 2.75 inches. Baltimore Checkerspots dazzle the eyes with their black base coloration, which sets off their densely packed, stunning orange-red and pale yellow wing spots. Their red-orange spots match the color of their feet, face and antennae clubs. There's simply no spot wasted on this butterfly that doesn't warn predators to leave it alone.

□ **Caterpillar:** Young caterpillars feed in the safety of a silken tent but, when they mature, display the classic warning coloration of a toxic animal—orange-red and black

A Baltimore Checkerspot shows off its underside. This toxic butterfly's striking pattern is meant as warning coloration to ward off predators.

Plant a drift of white turtlehead in that problematic wet place in your garden in northern areas, and be sure to eradicate lythrum, which threatens their habitat. Farther south, keep your woodlot free of exotic or dense brush that shades out the Checkerspot's other main host plant, wild false foxgloves. False foxgloves are uncultivatable because they are partially tree root parasites. Do not tidy up around known butterfly colonies, because the caterpillars must have leaf litter as shelter to overwinter. Plant butterflyweed as a favorite nectar source.

striped with branched black spines.

▫ **Chrysalis:** The bird-dropping-like chrysalis is somewhat like an unappetizing bird dropping—nevertheless stunning white with black and orange spots and marbling.

▫ **Local Relative:** Several species of similar checkerspots occur in the West. Variable Checkerspot (*Euphydryas chalcedona*) is your most likely garden visitor and resides throughout most of the West in open woodland country. Western Indian paintbrushes, monkeyflowers and penstemons are host plants, and its favorite nectar sources are yellow composites like marguerites and coreopsis. The butterfly varies somewhat in appearance from one place to another and there are many named subspecies—hence the appropriate common name.

A Baltimore Checkerspot with wings outspread, nectaring on red clover.

Question Mark
Polygonia interrogationis

If you're ever asked about how this butterfly got its name, just look at its underside hind wing and you will see a most familiar mark—a question-mark-like metallic marking! Question Marks are in a group of butterflies that are cryptic, bark-like or leaf-like with their wings closed, and orange with black speckles and dark borders above. They are called anglewings for their obvious angular wing edges.

Anglewings all look pretty much the same and this may be a form of mimicry to give the same message to would-be predators. All of these butterflies fly extremely fast in an erratic, hard-to-follow path, so are almost impossible for birds to catch. After a bird wastes a lot of energy trying to catch one, it will not bother again. The message is "you can't catch me," so these butterflies are usually just left alone.

▫ **Status:** A resident butterfly that overwinters as a butterfly; many adults move southward to overwinter.

▫ **Habitat:** Anyplace with trees—forests, woodlands, hedgerows and other disturbed areas like tree-filled yards and gardens.

▫ **Garden Habit:** Question Marks are a regular visitor to the butterfly feeder or to fallen fruit from your favorite fruit tree. Otherwise, they seem to just hang out and bask in the sunshine and only occasionally do they visit flowers. In fall they seek out hollow trees or wood and brushpiles to overwinter in.

▫ **Garden Nectar Plants:** Often listed as not visiting flowers—but this is not true—though it nectars mainly on white, pinkish or purplish flowers: shrubs: butterfly bush, summersweet clethra; perennials: milkweeds, asters,

The silvery white mark on the hind wing identifies the Question Mark butterfly.

A summer-form Question Mark.

chrysanthemums; annual: *Verbena bonariensis*.

▫ **Garden Host Plants:** large trees: elms, hackberry, sugarberry; vine: hops; weed: nettles.

▫ **Identification:** 2.25 to 3 inches. The Question Mark has sharply angled forewings and pointed hind wings. It looks very leaf-like with its wings closed—its hind wing is punctuated with its namesake—a metallic silver question mark. The upper sides of warm-season, summer butterflies have mostly black hind wings, while cool-season-form (fall-winter-spring) butterflies have speckled orange hind wings.

Plant a sugarberry or hackberry as a shade tree to host this butterfly. Make sure to have some hollow trees, dead wood or a brushpile in which Question Marks may hibernate. Install a butterfly feeder containing overripe fruit, or leave some fruit from your favorite fruit tree unharvested.

The upper side wings of both forms are edged in lavender which wears off as the butterfly ages.

▫ **Caterpillar:** Question Mark caterpillars are black with various highlights and a row of branched spines on each of the caterpillar's segments. They often feed in groups and can defoliate seedling or sapling hackberry trees.

▫ **Chrysalis:** The greenish brown chrysalis has sharp points on its abdomen and a humped back with a saddle of silver in between.

▫ **Similar Species:** See Eastern Comma and related commas.

A newly emerged, cool-season-form Question Mark is edged in lavender.

Eastern Comma

Polygonia comma

The Eastern Comma and all comma butterflies are named precisely in the same manner as the Question Mark—for their metallic marking on their underside hind wing. On these butterflies this mark is in the shape of another punctuation mark: the comma.

Eastern Comma is so named because it is the most prevalent comma in the eastern half of the continent. It has another name you may run across, "Hop Merchant"—presumably because this butterfly's caterpillars feed on hop vines and were probably a pest interfering in the trade of growing hops for making beer. Commas are in the anglewing group of butterflies, so sometimes are referred to as "Comma Anglewings."

Eastern Comma is the butterfly you are most likely to cross paths with in winter anywhere in its range. It overwinters as an adult butterfly and emerges on mild winter days to bask and fly about the woods, more so than any other butterfly.

The underside of the Eastern Comma is patterned and colored to look like bark. The silvery white comma-like mark on its hind wing is characteristic of several species of comma butterflies.

□ **Status:** Eastern Comma (and all commas) is a hardy resident butterfly that overwinters as a butterfly. Eastern Comma is a stray butterfly beyond the southwestern portion of its range in Colorado and Texas.

□ **Habitat:** Commas are butterflies of forests, woodlands and wooded towns, cities and suburbs. There must be trees present for commas to roost on.

□ **Garden Habit:** Eastern Commas roost among tree trunks where they blend in perfectly with the bark. They seldom visit flowers. Commas will appear from nowhere and visit your butterfly feeder of overripe fruit. You may oftentimes have Eastern Commas feeding alongside Question Marks and other species of commas, depending on where you're located. They will imbibe moisture from a bare wet spot in the yard and otherwise just perch and bask throughout the yard, including on your patio deck and house—they are actually waiting for passing potential mates.

□ **Garden Nectar Plants:** Sap, dung, overripe fruit and moisture nourish Eastern Commas. Satyr and Hoary Commas do visit flowers.

The Hoary Comma looks nearly identical to the Eastern Comma but is found only in the far North and the cool, mountainous West.

□ **Garden Host Plants:** shade tree: American elm; perennial vine: hops; weedy plants: those in the nettle family.

□ **Identification:** 2 to 2.5 inches. Eastern Comma has angled wings, not quite as dramatically edged nor as pointed as those of the Question Mark. They are more grayish brown on their underside and their hind wing is punctuated with their namesake metallic silver comma mark. The upper sides of summer-form butterflies have dark hind wings, while fall-winter-spring butterflies have speckled orange hind wings.

□ **Caterpillar:** The caterpillars are spiny but vary in color from black to greenish brown or whitish. Older caterpillars feed at night under their shelter of a leaf whose edges they've drawn together using their silk.

This cool-season form of the Eastern Comma is feasting on a fallen pear.

TIPS
TO ATTRACT

A butterfly feeder filled with overripe fruit is a sure bet to attract this butterfly to yards with trees. Plant or neglect a patch of nettles in a secluded weedy nook to host Eastern Comma and several other butterflies. Unfortunately for humans, most species of nettles have stinging hairs on them that can be very annoying—but at least the pain goes away rather quickly. (But nettles don't cause dermatitis as poison ivy does.)

□ **Chrysalis:** The brownish chrysalis is similar to Question Mark with a gold or silver saddle between its humped back and thorny abdomen.

□ **Local Relatives:** Satyr Comma (*Polygonia satyrus*) is the most widespread of the other commas found in gardens. It was formerly called Golden Anglewing, or just Satyr, and is the most golden colored comma. Gray Comma (*Polygonia progne*) is well named for its uniformly gray bark-like pattern beneath. It is the second most widespread comma. Green Comma (*Polygonia faunus*) and Hoary Comma (*Polygonia gracilis*) are two other prevalent western and northern species.

An Eastern Comma (top view) gathers salts.

Mourning Cloak

Nymphalis antiopa

This cloak is not one of sadness and grieving, but relates to the thrill of observing something marvelously beautiful. In England, where this butterfly is known as the "Camberwell Beauty," it is treasured because it so rarely strays there. Mourning Cloaks have a vast range—residing in mainland Europe, Asia and in North America southward to Venezuela in South America. It inhabits a wide zone of climates too—from semitropical to tundra.

Mourning Cloak is another winter butterfly and is often encountered out basking, flying and gliding on sunny, mild winter days even in the cold Canadian region. It is amazing how impervious they are to cold, since they overwinter in areas where the temperature can drop to -50°F. The Mourning Cloak is one of our longest living butterflies.

They readily live almost a full year as an adult butterfly—but they spend much of their life in hibernation through the winter months, waiting for some warm days in which to flit about and surprise human viewers.

▫ **Status:** A long-lived resident butterfly that overwinters as an adult; some fly southward or to lower elevations to overwinter. A rare wintering stray butterfly in most of Florida and south Texas (and even Bermuda!).

▫ **Habitat:** Mourning Cloaks are butterflies of deciduous forests, woodlands and wooded cities, towns and suburbs. The butterfly widely disperses so can be found in open country on occasion.

▫ **Garden Habit:** Mourning Cloaks usually just glide through the garden and appear to move on. They will stop to feed at a butterfly feeder filled with overripe fruit or

A Mourning Cloak with its wings closed looks like a piece of bark. This helps the butterfly hide during hibernation.

Put up that butterfly feeder and keep it well stocked with fruit and watermelon slices. Leave fallen logs and deadwood where appropriate or build a brushpile to create a wintering site. Be sure to look over firewood brought in from outside and release any hibernating Mourning Cloaks you've disturbed.

watermelon. They rarely stop to nectar on garden flowers. In fall they search for hibernaclea (places to hibernate)—dead wood, hollows, a brushpile or firewood, as places to overwinter in. If your garden hosts Mourning Cloaks, be prepared to feed an army—the caterpillars are gregarious and can defoliate plants.

❑ **Garden Nectar Plants:** shrubs: butterfly bush, New Jersey tea; perennial: milkweeds; weedy plant: dogbane.

❑ **Garden Host Plants:** Feeds on a wide array of plants: large trees: paper birch, hackberry, quaking aspen, cottonwoods, willows, elms; small trees: mulberries, plums; shrubs: wild roses, blackberries, willows.

❑ **Identification:** 3.25 to 4 inches. A medium-large butterfly that is unmistakable. Its upper side is rich chestnut brown with an outer band of blue spots and a white or cream margin to the jagged-edged wings. The underside is cryptic gray and black to make it look like bark.

❑ **Caterpillar:** The black caterpillar is armed with branched spines and dotted with tiny white spots. It has contrasting red spots on its back and red prolegs. The gregarious caterpillars can feed in an army and defoliate their host and then wander to unrelated adjacent plantings to feed.

❑ **Chrysalis:** The more or less brown-gray chrysalis has two points on its head, a humped back and pinkish-tipped spines on its abdomen.

❑ **Local Relatives:** See Tortoiseshells.

A Mourning Cloak basks on a black-eyed Susan. Mourning Cloaks seldom nectar on flowers.

Gallery of Tortoiseshells

COMPTON TORTOISESHELL

Nymphalis vaualbum (2.75 to 3.35 inches)

Compton Tortoiseshell is named after Compton County, Quebec, not after a person. It is a resident butterfly that overwinters as an adult butterfly—often in a group in a hollow tree or beneath the bark of a dead tree, and occasionally in vacant sheds or cabins. The butterfly is long lived—living at least nine months—but it hibernates for much of this time.

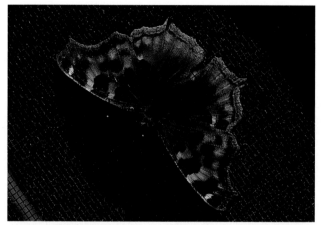

A Compton Tortoiseshell basks on the screen of a northern lodge in Ontario, Canada.

During years when they are abundant, these tortoiseshells occasionally stray to both the north and south of their home in the northwoods and northern Rocky Mountain forests. They are a butterfly of many of our summer vacations along a lake "up north." In the spring, the newly awakened butterflies nectar on willow flowers, feed on sap and drink moisture from wet mud. They will venture into gardens adjacent to wooded habitat, where they will visit butterfly feeders of overripe fruit but ignore flowers.

Compton Tortoiseshells can be identified by their angled wings—but are larger than all the anglewings. They are gray below with a cryptic bark-like pattern to perfectly blend in with tree trunks. Above, they are rich, chestnut brown blending to golden orange with black patches and a white spot at the upper corner of each wing. Their host plants include aspens, birches and willow trees.

MILBERT'S TORTOISESHELL

Nymphalis milberti (2 to 2.5 inches)

Milbert's Tortoiseshell is named after one Mr. Milbert, who collected North American butterflies in 1826 and whose collection currently resides at the Museum of Natural His-

tory in Paris, France. This tortoiseshell is a resident butterfly that, like its cousins, overwinters as an adult. It is a wide-ranging butterfly—found across the northern half of the continent in meadows, flowery fields and prairies among woodlands and even taiga and alpine areas. It is a rare stray southward.

Milbert's Tortoiseshells are avid flower visitors and will nectar at blooming lilacs and thistles but are especially attracted to autumn-blooming asters and goldenrods. They readily visit gardens near open country.

Milbert's Tortoiseshell is easily identified. They are black above with two warm bands of yellow blending outward to orange along all four wings, with blue spots along their black wing margins. Their underside is two-toned—black from the body to midwing, then cryptic scaly gray and black on the outer half of the wing. These tortoiseshells' host plants are nettles, where the young caterpillars feed gregariously in a silken tent of their own creation. Older caterpillars feed alone, sheltered in leaves they have folded over themselves.

A Milbert's Tortoiseshell nectaring with its wings outspread on a frost aster.

CALIFORNIA TORTOISESHELL

Nymphalis californica (2.25 to 2.75 inches)

California Tortoiseshell is a resident and colonist butterfly of California, the Pacific Northwest and the Rocky Mountains. It is a butterfly of chaparral and open woodlands, and is most common in the central part of its namesake state, northward into Washington, where it overwinters as a butterfly. It also overwinters as a butterfly along the front range of the Rocky Mountains. Some California butterflies actually perform a sort of migration—from overwintering in the Coast Ranges and Sierra foothills they spread eastward to the high Sierras and beyond. Three broods later, they may return to overwinter.

Some years this butterfly goes through massive population explosions, and butterflies move en masse in a north and eastward emigration. During these events in California, they can be hit by cars in such numbers that they litter the highway and cause vehicles to skid. A few stray butterflies may rarely blow far to the east.

California Tortoiseshells are mostly orange on their upper side with black margins and some black patches centered on the forewing and with a white spot near the apex of the forewing. The underside is cryptic brown with a tree-bark-like pattern. The California Tortoiseshell's host plants are wild lilacs. The caterpillars are gregarious when young and do not create any nests or protections around themselves.

A Milbert's Tortoiseshell displays its bark-like underside while nectaring on the blossoms of New England aster.

Two California Tortoiseshells take a drink.

American Lady

Vanessa virginiensis

The American Lady is one of our most stunningly colored and patterned butterflies! A newly emerged butterfly, when viewed nectaring with its wings closed, displays the American Lady at her best. The marvelously marbled undersides show hues of black, white, beige, taupe, periwinkle and pink—all with violet highlights and two circular spots on the hind wing. The cosmopolitan (world-wide) Painted Lady cannot hold a candle to the beauty of this American butterfly, which is a totally different animal. (I learned to distinguish them at a very young age—5—and never thought of them as confusing species.)

American Lady was formerly known as the "American Painted Lady." West Coast Lady and Red Admiral are also close cousins in the "lady" clan. American Lady is the hardiest of the bunch and doesn't have the wild population swings that the other ladies undergo.

▫ **Status:** American Lady is a resident butterfly of moist mild-winter zones. It colonizes much of North America in summer. The exact range between resident and colonist populations is unknown or disputed and may vary from year to year depending on the severity of the winter.

▫ **Habitat:** American Ladies inhabit all sorts of open country filled with wildflowers—from open woods and woodland edges to savannas, prairies, meadows, roadsides, yards and

Butterfly bush is a great summertime nectar plant for Painted Ladies.

gardens.

▫ **Garden Habit:** The first American Ladies of spring invade the garden to nectar on chives and even dandelions. In summer, they linger around the garden, nectaring on butterfly bushes, marigolds, Mexican sunflowers and zinnias. In fall, expect American Ladies on single chrysanthemums and select asters. Their caterpillars can become a nuisance and defoliate some cherished silvery-leaved plants.

▫ **Garden Nectar Plants:** shrubs: butterfly bush, buttonbush, summersweet clethra, garden lilacs; perennials: chives, milkweeds, asters, chrysanthemums, mountain mints; biennial: thistles; annuals: marigolds, Mexican sunflower, zinnias; weedy plants: winter cress, dogbanes and vetches.

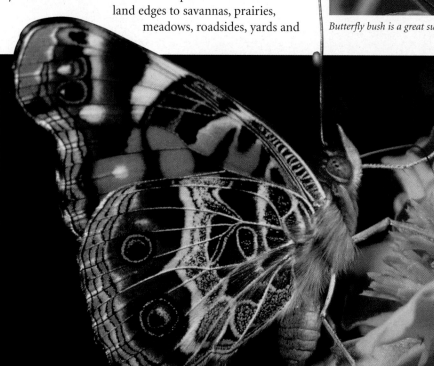

An American Lady nectars on a single-flowered marigold.

Helichrysum and dusty millers—two silvery, hairy-foliaged plants grown throughout the country—often host American Lady caterpillars, which can defoliate the plants. Plant low-growing pussytoes mixed with other low ground-covers to host American Ladies—pussytoes' low-growing nature hides the foliage-ruining effects of hungry American Lady caterpillars. Blooming chives are a magnet to the first-brood butterflies—setting the stage for the butterflies to colonize your garden through the summer. Remember to remove your chives' spent flowers, or they'll seed themselves obnoxiously.

▫ **Garden Host Plants:** gray-haired, "silvery" plants, as: perennials: pearly everlastings, pussytoes, sweet everlastings and related cudweeds; annuals: helichrysums and dusty millers.

▫ **Identification:** 2.25 to 2.5 inches. The best field mark to correctly identify an American Lady from the Painted Lady and the West Coast Lady is its two pronounced circular spots on the underside hind wing.

▫ **Caterpillar:** The caterpillars feed in nests they've built by using their silk to connect plant fragments. The caterpillars are yellow with black bands—the bands contain reddish-based, branched spines with white spots between them.

▫ **Chrysalis:** The chrysalises match their surroundings, cryptic green or gray.

An American Painted Lady.

Painted Lady

Vanessa cardui

Painted Ladies are also known as the thistle butterfly and the cosmopolitan. The butterflies love to nectar on thistle blossoms, and the caterpillars munch the spiny foliage as a favorite host plant. The huge range of the butterfly encompasses much of the Earth, from Europe, Asia and Africa to all of North America—so the butterfly's cosmopolitan name makes a lot of sense.

In spring, Painted Ladies emerge en masse from the deserts of northern Mexico and fly northward on the warm winds of spring. When they encounter an obstacle, their northward beeline does not waiver—they simply fly over the obstruction. Thousands of butterflies partake in these occasional mass flights but, most years, Painted Ladies don't occur in such numbers. The Painted Lady colonizes much of North America by summer and even somehow finds the island of Bermuda!

New broods increase the emigrant northern populations, which simply die in the cold of winter. It is hard for us to grasp their reason for being, knowing that all these emigrant butterflies, including their caterpillars, chrysalises and eggs, will die every winter—only those from the South will repopulate next year. Painted Ladies are the only but-terfly commercially in the toy trade—you can purchase kits to raise them, and they are not governed by interstate transport laws.

▫ **Status:** Painted Ladies are a nearly worldwide colonist and resident only in semitropical regions.

▫ **Habitat:** A butterfly fond of thistles, the Painted Lady occurs in disturbed areas where most thistles grow. Vacant old fields, roadsides, abandoned lots and meadows are favorite habitats. Many native thistles occur in more pristine habitat, like open woods and prairies, and the butter-flies do likewise.

▫ **Garden Habit:** The numbers of Painted Ladies visiting the garden varies from year to year. They are usually seen nectaring on spring flowers—they especially like blooming chives, just like American Ladies, and visit butterfly bushes and various perennials for nectar in midsummer and fall.

▫ **Garden Nectar Plants:** shrubs: butterfly bush, button-bush, lilacs; perennials: milkweeds, asters, chrysanthe-mums, purple coneflowers, globe thistles, Joe-Pye-weeds, blazingstars, ironweeds; biennial: thistles; annuals: cosmos, zinnias; weedy plants: mustards, clovers.

▫ **Garden Host Plants:** a wide variety of plants but espe-

The Painted Lady is one of the most cosmopolitan of all butterflies: It is found nearly worldwide.

Plant ornamental thistles! Nearly all native thistles are not the invasive exotic weeds we know as thistles, and are really beautiful plants. A good identification rule of thumb is, if there's a white felty underside to the leaf, then it's a native thistle. *Do not plant* Nodding Thistle, Bull Thistle and Canada Thistle (not native to Canada) or any other non-native thistle—these are the noxious pests. Globe thistle (which is not a true thistle) is a substitute for the faint of heart, and the Painted Ladies like it just the same.

cially thistles, hollyhocks and mallows.

▫ **Identification:** 2.25 to 2.75 inches. Painted Ladies have a similar pattern to American Ladies and West Coast Ladies, but differ from the prior by their bold black flecks above, and golden (not taupe) marbled underside with a series of small eyes near the hind wing margin. West Coast Ladies have strongly squared-off wing tips and have blue jeweled eye spots along the underside's hind wing.

▫ **Caterpillar:** Caterpillars feed alone, encased in a silken web tied among the host plant's foliage. They are quite variable in coloration, from gray to brown to black, armored with many branched spines.

▫ **Chrysalis:** The pale chrysalis is shiny grayish or brownish with golden-tipped pointed bumps.

A Painted Lady displays its underside. This specimen is busy nectaring on zinnias.

West Coast Lady

Vanessa annabella

This well-named relative to the American and Painted Ladies is the most common butterfly in the lowlands of our most populous state: California. The butterfly resides year-round only in the mildest coastal zones as far north as Vancouver Island, British Columbia.

West Coast Lady has a colonization spirit like that of the Painted Lady but strikes out on an eastward course. This butterfly colonizes much of the West—more so some years than others—occasionally straying all the way to the edge of the Great Plains. Why a butterfly undergoes colonization of new ranges in summer is little understood. Why bother, when all the new colonists will die when winter comes? These butterflies may be poised to take advantage of climate change. Perceived global warming may expand the resident ranges of these species or ensure their long-term survival. If their current resident ranges become unsuitable, while their colonist range becomes mild enough for them to overwinter, they are also likely to flourish. For whatever

reason, cold-winter gardeners should celebrate all the beauty these emigrant butterflies bring to summer gardens.

❑ **Status:** West Coast Ladies are resident butterflies that are present all year in the Mediterranean climate of California. They are also residents of the coastal areas of the Pacific Northwest, where they overwinter as a chrysalis. They are irregular colonists in the desert Southwest, Great Basin and Rocky Mountains.

❑ **Habitat:** West Coast Lady resides in various open lands from open woods, grasslands and meadows to roadsides, yards and gardens.

❑ **Garden Habit:** West Coast Ladies are avid flower nectarers and reside in the garden nearly year-round. They are easy to raise on their host plants outdoors or indoors. A good project for a child—to care for and to watch their miraculous metamorphosis process.

❑ **Garden Nectar Plants:** shrubs: abelias, escallonia, rabbitbrush, lantana (California, Arizona), plumbago; perennials:

A West Coast Lady nectars on rabbitbrush.

asters, Jupiter's beard; annuals: bur marigolds, lantana.
- **Garden Host Plants:** perennials: hollyhocks, checkermallows, common mallow.
- **Identification:** 2 to 2.25 inches. West Coast Lady has a strongly squared-off wing tip unlike that of other Ladies. On the upper side, the white spotting on the forewings is limited to the outermost tip and the hind wing is mostly orange with the blue-jewel centered black spots—which are also the primary field mark on the butterfly's underside.
- **Caterpillar:** The caterpillars are variable in color and live inside a silken nest they've spun among the leaves.
- **Chrysalis:** The chrysalis is light brown with golden spots, similar to that of the Painted Lady.
- **Local Relative:** Kameamea Lady (*V. tameamea*) is one of two butterflies native to Hawaii. Painted Ladies, American Ladies and Red Admirals have all been introduced into Hawaii.

The West Coast Lady has strongly squared-off wing tips and a row of blue, jewel-like spots on its hind wings.

Red Admiral

Vanessa atalanta

The Red Admiral is actually closely related to the "lady" butterflies and not the admirals, so should really be called the red lady.

Red Admirals undergo periodic spring population explosions, where thousands of butterflies may emerge and fill the landscape with butterflies. Mass movements of these butterflies fly northward, but most years there are just single butterflies emigrating. The massive fluctuations in population of this and other butterflies is not well understood—possibly there is an abundance of the host plant certain years—but the Red Admiral's host, the weedy nettle plant, doesn't vary in abundance from year to year. There probably is a parasite or disease that attacks when the butterflies are abundant and is in remission when the butterflies are scarce.

□ **Status:** Red Admiral is a resident butterfly in mild-winter regions where it overwinters as a caterpillar or chrysalis. It is a colonist in all other zones, sometimes surviving mild winters.

□ **Habitat:** Red Admirals are most common along flood-plain forests, where their host plant, nettles, abound. Nettles grow in various moist, disturbed woodlands, and Red Admirals are notoriously wide ranging, so the butterfly is found almost anywhere.

□ **Garden Habit:** Red Admirals are skittish, fast fliers, but also pugnacious and territorial. They may buzz around you when you walk by and often chase other butterflies from their favorite domains. They can be bullies and physically usurp any other butterfly that competes for their choice food sources.

□ **Garden Nectar Plants:** Red Admirals have a taste for tree sap and overripe fruit and avidly visit butterfly feeders. Small trees: early flowering fruit trees, as peaches and plums; shrubs: abelias, butterfly bush, rabbit-brush, summersweet clethra, garden lilacs; perennials: asters, Jupiter's beard, chrysanthemums, milkweeds, purple coneflowers; weedy plants: dogbane and clovers.

□ **Garden Host Plants:** weedy plants: those in the nettle family.

□ **Identification:** 2.25 to 3 inches. With their wings open, Red Admirals are easily identified by their forewing's carmine red band, which ties into a same-colored marginal band on the hind wing. There are a few white speckles near the forewing wing tip. The underside hind wing is marbled with black and gray in fine detail, and the underside forewing, which extends beyond the hind wing, shows some bright colors, from rose pink to blue and white.

□ **Caterpillar:** Red Admiral caterpillars are mostly black (occasionally pale) with a row

A Red Admiral deserves a closer look at the fine details of its underside.

TIPS
TO ATTRACT

A butterfly feeder is a must to attract Red Admirals. Plant 'Magnus' purple coneflower, or any other of its cultivars, or its refined wild form, to attract a pugnacious Red Admiral.

of whitish spots along the sides, and red-based, black barbed spines on each segment of the caterpillar. Young caterpillars fold a leaf over themselves, using their silk to create a sheltered fort to feed in—as they grow older, they create a multi-leaf shelter. These shelters on nettles make them easy to locate.

□ **Chrysalis:** The chrysalis is gray with gold-tipped "cleats" on its back.

A Red Admiral displays open wings, banded in carmine red, while it takes nectar from a butterfly bush.

Common Buckeye

Junonia coenia

The Common Buckeye is our most fabulously patterned butterfly, with large, colorful fake eye spots and fine iridescent details. (Its underside is dull by comparison.) Anyone in a region with warm summers can count on this butterfly to beautify their gardens.

Common Buckeye is certainly more beautiful than any buck's eye. It is a summer colonist to Ohio (the Buckeye State) and has nothing to do with the wild horsechestnut trees called buckeyes—hopefully "buck" is in the context of "cheer up!"

The false eye spots are surprisingly cryptic when the butterfly lies in the grass, but the markings are probably meant to spook would-be predators—even if only for that split second buckeyes need for an escape. Buckeyes are fiercely territorial and check out and chase all intruders—even larger butterflies.

❑ **Status:** Common Buckeye is a resident only in nearly frost-free zones of the Southwest and Southeast, where it survives as an adult butterfly or as a chrysalis. It is a regular colonist northward through much of the warm-summer regions of the continent.

❑ **Habitat:** The Common Buckeye prefers disturbed open grasslands—especially where there is some bare ground. They can be found on roadsides, railroads, abandoned lots and open woods, savannas, dunes and other dry grasslands and prairies. They can be common in gardens with lawns and flower borders.

❑ **Garden Habit:** Buckeyes are a bit skittish until they get to know you. When startled, they fly rapidly away on swift wing beats and long glides. Once they're accustomed to

A Common Buckeye prepares to nectar on a globe amaranth.

The White Peacock is a buckeye relative that inhabits South Florida and Texas but is commonly found in captivity at butterfly houses across the country.

your actions, they nectar with their wings widespread—showing off their beauty. They are very territorial and investigate other butterflies that intrude on their domain.

❑ **Garden Nectar Plants:** shrubs: coyote brush, seepwillow, groundsel bush, butterfly bushes; perennials: asters, chrysanthemums; annuals: sulphur cosmos, *Verbena bonariensis*.

❑ **Garden Host Plants:** lots of plants in the snapdragon, plantain, vervain and acanthus families; the most garden-worthy plants being perennial: butter-and-eggs and flaxes; annual: snapdragons; weedy plant: lawn plantains.

❑ **Identification:** 1.5 to 2.75 inches. Buckeyes are unmistakable except in semitropical areas where a few similar species may occur. You can easily observe their brown wings with six large, beautiful eye spots and a creamy band on the forewing—even in flight. The underside is pale tannish brown with darker lines in spring and summer, and rosy brown in fall broods that overwinter. The pale forewing band and large eye spot are visible on the underside of both forms.

❑ **Caterpillar:** The black-and-cream caterpillar has orange markings and exhibits branched spines on each segment.

Plant a border of mixed orange sulphur cosmos interspersed with tall, airy violet-blue *Verbena bonariensis*—both of these nectar-rich plants are first choices for buckeyes and are self-sowing, so will return year after year. Edge your planting with low, pale yellow snapdragons to provide a host plant—snapdragons bloom only in spring or fall in hot-summer climates (winter in mildest zones). These plants ensure a resident gang of buckeyes.

◻ **Chrysalis:** The marbly white chrysalis shows an eye spot on its wing case. It looks somewhat like a bird dropping.

◻ **Local Relative:** White Peacock is a common butterfly of peninsular Florida and south Texas gardens. White Peacocks are usually found near water, where their hosts—frogfruits, water ruellias and water bacopa grow. They nectar on lantanas and shepherd's needle. Butterflies found farther north have probably hitched a ride on plant shipments from Florida, as their host plants have become popular water garden plants—other northern butterflies have probably escaped—they do well in captivity and are often on display at butterfly houses across the country.

The spectacularly beautiful eye spots on a Common Buckeye serve a startling stare to any would-be predator.

Viceroy
Limenitis archippus

Viceroys mimic the Monarch and Queen, depending on which one is the more common resident in their region. They do this to gain protection from predators. "Queen" Viceroys are brownish orange and "Monarch" Viceroys are orange. Birds that eat a toxic Monarch or Queen get sick and learn never to mess with butterflies with such coloration and pattern! Birds cannot tell the difference between the Monarch and the Viceroy.

Recent research has learned that Viceroys may be distasteful too—they feed on willows, which are the original source of aspirin. If this is the case, then both the Monarchs and Viceroys benefit from each other's similar looks.

Interestingly, Viceroys are not closely related to Monarchs and are actually in a group of butterflies called admirals. Their first cousin, the Red-Spotted Purple, is also a

This Viceroy, with outspread wings, differs from the Monarch by having a black line crossing the black-lined veins of its hind wing.

Verbena bonariensis, *an annual, is a favorite Viceroy nectar plant.*

mimic, and their western relative, the Lorquin's Admiral, also looks like another butterfly.

▫ **Status:** Viceroys are a hardy resident butterfly that survives the winter as a young caterpillar safely wrapped in a rolled leaf permanently attached to a twig by their silk.

▫ **Habitat:** Viceroys are seldom far from their willow hosts, which are most common on the banks of rivers and streams and in swales and wetlands.

▫ **Garden Habit:** Viceroys act very different from Monarchs in the garden. Viceroys' flap-glide flight helps identify them from the buoyant soars of the Monarch. Viceroys' taste in flowers is quite different from that of Monarchs—their nectar choices show a preference for white flowers and no milkweeds.

▫ **Garden Nectar Plants:** visitor to butterfly feeder; shrub: butterfly bush (especially white ones!); perennials: asters, Joe-Pye-weeds, rattlesnake masters, mountain mints, black-eyed Susans, goldenrods; annual: *Verbena bonariensis.*

▫ **Garden Host Plants:** large trees: cottonwoods, willows; shrub: willows.

▫ **Identification:** 2.75 to 3.25 inches. Viceroys are orange or brown-orange butterflies with white-spotted black wing margins and black veining, just

A butterfly feeder filled with overripe fruit or a slice of watermelon is a great treat for a Viceroy. Plant a willow for Viceroys to host on. Willows can be vigorous weedy trees, so cut them back to the ground or any suitable height annually to provide succulent new shoots for the Viceroy caterpillars to feed on. Remember not to destroy their winter hibernation leaf if you cut in the dormant season. White-flowering 'White Bouquet' and 'White Profusion' or pale purple-flowering 'Lochinch' cultivars of butterfly bush are favorite nectar sources.

like a Monarch. They have a distinctive "field mark" line across the middle of their hind wing.

❑ **Caterpillar:** Viceroy caterpillars mimic bird droppings to avoid being eaten by predators—they are a remarkable mimic, even appearing wet for a fresh look! The caterpillars have two dark twig-like horns on the second segment behind their head and often tuck their head under with these two "horns" pointing forward. Young caterpillars overwinter in a tightly rolled leaf attached to a twig by their silk. All the other admirals' caterpillars are nearly identical to the Viceroy's caterpillar.

❑ **Chrysalis:** Viceroy chrysalises are characteristically hump-backed and also mimic a bird dropping.

A Viceroy rests with its wings closed beneath the bird-dropping-like chrysalis of another Viceroy.

White Admiral & Red-Spotted Purple

Limenitis arthemis

White Admiral

Red-Spotted Purple

The White Admiral and the Red-Spotted Purple are two subspecies of the same butterfly. The Red-Spotted Purple (*astyanax*) is the more widespread and southerly, while White Admiral (*arthemis*) is a denizen of the northwoods. If you live where the two subspecies overlap, you may encounter both subspecies, or butterflies that look like a blend between the two.

Red-Spotted Purples look the way they do to mimic the Pipevine Swallowtail, which is distasteful to birds. Birds learn not to eat any butterfly that is black with shiny blue highlights.

Red-Spotted Purples are named for this bluish or greenish "purple" sheen and for their underside spots of red. The White Admiral is exactly the same but has a broad white band through the middle of each of the wings that is visible from both above and below. The underside red spots are in exactly the same place as are those of the Red-Spotted Purple. Pipevine Swallowtails don't inhabit their northerly range, so mimicking one makes no sense.

White Admirals and Red-Spotted Purples are close relatives to the Viceroy, Weidemeyer's and Lorquin's Admiral, and there are records of hybrids between any of them wherever their ranges overlap. White Admirals/Red-Spotted Purples usually perch on a sunny shrub or branch and wait for passing potential mates. They fly with alternating flaps and long glides characteristic of the whole admiral clan. They search the forest

The red spots of the Red-Spotted Purple are apparent only on its underside.

for sap, dung or overripe fruit as nourishment and often imbibe moisture from wet spots and puddle edges. They only occasionally visit flowers for nectar.

▫ **Status:** These admirals are a resident butterfly that survives the winter as a young caterpillar. Red-Spotted Purple is also a stray west of its range in the southern Great Plains.

▫ **Habitat:** These admirals are denizens of woodlands, forests and wooded urban areas. They are never found far from trees. White Admiral graces northeastern mixed forests while Red-Spotted Purples inhabit central, southern and southwestern hardwood forests and woodlands (and their associated urban forests).

▫ **Garden Habit:** Red-Spotted Purple and White Admirals glide through the understory or lower canopy of your woods or lawn trees. They descend into the garden to visit butterfly feeders, and their few choice nectaring plants—butterfly bush and purple coneflowers—are about their only two nectar sources in the flower border. Once they've

The Red-Spotted Purple favors white blossoms like this butterfly bush. The butterfly's coloration mimics that of the distasteful Pipevine Swallowtail.

clethra, spirea, viburnums; perennial: purple coneflower.

□ **Garden Host Plants:** White Admiral: large trees: yellow birch, sweet birch, aspens; Red-Spotted Purple: large trees: cottonwoods, poplars, black cherry, black oak; small tree: chokecherry.

□ **Identification:** 3 to 4 inches. Red-Spotted Purples are a tailless butterfly that is predominantly black with a bluish or greenish sheen on its hind wings and red spots below. White Admiral is the only predominantly black butterfly with bold white bands on its wings in the East. In the West, it is similar to Weidemeyer's Admiral, but White Admiral displays a bluish or greenish sheen on its hind wings.

□ **Caterpillar:** Their caterpillar is nearly identical in looks and habits to the Viceroy—identify them by what food plant you find them on or by which one's range you're in.

□ **Chrysalis:** Their chrysalis is nearly identical to the Viceroy's—bird-dropping-like with the same characteristic humped back.

covered your treasures, they often take up territory and residence in your yard or garden, and you can enjoy their presence for several days.

□ **Garden Nectar Plants:** large tree: basswoods; small tree: devil's walkingstick; shrubs: butterfly bush, summersweet

The aptly named White Admiral, the northern race of the Red-Spotted Purple, lives where there are no Pipevine Swallowtails to mimic.

Lorquin's Admiral & Weidemeyer's Admiral

Limenitis lorquini and *Limenitis weidemeyerii*

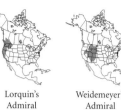

Lorquin's Admiral   Weidemeyer's Admiral

The northwestern Lorquin's Admiral, formerly "Orange-Tip Admiral" and the Rocky Mountain Weidemeyer's Admiral, formerly the "Western Admiral," are closely related to the Viceroy, White Admiral and Red-Spotted Purple. Admirals are all relatively the same size and shape, and their caterpillars and chrysalises are nearly identical. You can best differentiate their immature stages by what plant you find them on or by whose range you are in. They all have a characteristic flap-glide flight and really enliven woodlands across the country. They set

□ **Garden Habit:** Both species perch and await passing females. They are attracted to butterfly feeders with over-ripe fruit or cut melons.

□ **Garden Nectar Plants:** Lorquin's: small tree: California buckeye; shrubs: Yerba Santa, privets; Weidemeyer's: shrubs: seepwillow, snowberry, rabbitbrush; biennial: cow parsnip.

□ **Garden Host Plants:** large trees: quaking aspen, cottonwoods; small trees: domestic plums (L), apples (L), chokecherry; shrubs: ocean-sprays or rocksprays, willows, serviceberries (W), wild plums (L).

□ **Identification:** The Lorquin's Admiral (2 to 2.5 inches) and Weidemeyer's Admiral (3 to 3.74 inches) are both

A Lorquin's Admiral perches on a sunlit leaf.

up a territorial perch and are quite pugnacious—battling other butterflies or even chasing birds.

□ **Status:** These admirals are resident butterflies that over-winter as small caterpillars in their leaf shelter, just like the Viceroy and other admirals.

□ **Habitat:** Weidemeyer's Admiral inhabits drier forests in the central and southern Rocky Mountains, including wooded canyons, floodplain and streamside woodlands, open ponderosa pine lands, aspen groves and wooded urban areas and small towns. Lorquin's Admiral resides in the Pacific and northern Rocky Mountains in wooded mountain canyons, streamsides and floodplain woodlands, as well as marshes and wooded suburbs and towns.

A Weidemeyer's Admiral surveys its territory from a favorite perch.

TIPS
TO ATTRACT

To host these admirals, plant the locally native species of ocean-spray or rockspray shrubs, which have graceful, arching branches and fluffy white panicles of flowers. Put up a butterfly feeder filled with overripe fruit, or allow some fruit from your favorite fruit trees to go unharvested.

white-banded admirals—the Lorquin's Admiral looks as if its forewing tips were dipped in red-orange paint, while the Weidemeyer's Admiral is basically black and white above, with no bluish wash on the hind wing, as with White Admiral. Below, these beautifully patterned butterflies both show the white band, but Weidemeyer's is black with red highlights, while the Lorquin's Admiral underside base color is an exquisite orange-red.

▫ **Caterpillar:** Their caterpillars mimic a bird dropping and look just like the Viceroy caterpillar.

▫ **Chrysalis:** The chrysalis resembles a bird dropping and has the characteristic hump that all admiral butterflies do.

▫ **Local Relatives:** Lorquin's Admiral and the California Sister are look-alikes for unknown reasons. Weidemeyer's Admiral resembles the closely related White Admiral.

A Lorquin's Admiral nectars on a butterfly bush. Its orange-tipped wings help to identify it from the other admiral butterflies.

California Sister

Adelpha bredowii

The California Sister is a wanderer—it patrols for females and searches for overripe fruit or honeydew to feed on or mud to drink from. If a California Sister alights on a flower, then it's usually just perching there or basking in the sunshine and not nectaring. Incidentally, California Sister is named for its coloration, which is like that of a nun's habit, and for the state in which it commonly resides.

□ **Status:** California Sister is a resident butterfly in the Pacific Coast and southern Rocky Mountains, where it overwinters as a caterpillar. It is a stray into the intermountain region and eastward into the west edge of the southern Great Plains.

□ **Habitat:** The California Sister is found in oak savannas and oak woodlands and wanders far beyond, especially along streamside forests and into suburbs and towns.

□ **Garden Habit:** You often see California Sister backlit from below as it glides among the trees—its orange patch and white bands brilliantly engorged with color from the sun's rays. California Sister will visit the garden, sip from overripe fruit or moisture and only rarely from flower nec-

A California Sister showing the undersides of its wings.

tar. The butterfly's taste for fruit readily attracts it to wineries and other fruit-processing facilities.

□ **Garden Nectar Plants:** rarely nectars: small tree: California buckeye; shrubs: yellow and orange flowering species and cultivars of butterfly bushes, rabbitbrush and seepwillow.

□ **Garden Host Plants:** large trees: oaks, especially California live oak, canyon live oak, Arizona white oak, Emory oak, Gambel oak, golden chinkapin.

□ **Identification:** 2.5 to 4 inches. This brown butterfly, with white wing bands and forewings with an orange patch near their apex, closely resembles the Lorquin's Admiral, but the forewing tips have a black margin, so it looks more like an orange patch instead of orange tipped as with Lorquin's Admiral.

□ **Caterpillar:** The green and brown or yellow-orange and brown caterpillars, which have six pairs of tubercles on their back, construct a resting pad of silk and droppings (frass) at the end of a leaf vein.

□ **Chrysalis:** The chrysalis is

A California Sister soaking up some sunshine.

T I P S
TO ATTRACT

Plant and protect native oaks as shade trees in your yard, as host plant for the California Sister. Put up a butterfly feeder with overripe fruit and have a water garden or birdbath that has a wet stone or wet soil for California Sisters to drink from.

not as hump-backed as the admiral's and is pale yellow with golden spots on its back and two horns on its head.

□ **Local Relative:** There is no prevalent close relative, but the California Sister and the Lorquin's Admiral mimic each other for unknown reasons. You really have to take a second look to ascertain which species you're looking at.

A California Sister perched on California poppies. California Sisters seldom nectar on flowers.

Hackberry Emperor & Tawny Emperor

Asterocampa celtis and *Asterocampa clyton*

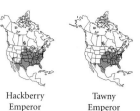

Hackberry Emperor   Tawny Emperor

These ubiquitous emperors should be called the friendly butterflies, as they will often land on your skin or your clothing to sample your sweat or perfume. Their spastic, fast flight makes them very difficult to observe until they land, and they are not above landing right on your nose.

What these butterflies lack in striking coloration they have in personality. Hackberry Emperors are far more common, and during many years they emerge in early summer by the thousands! Woodland roads become a challenge to drive without hitting hundreds. Tawny Emperors live side by side with Hackberry Emperors and act the same but emerge in consistently low to moderate numbers. These emperors are oblivious of each other and will readily share a butterfly feeder.

□ **Status:** Emperors are resident butterflies that overwinter as caterpillars attached to leaves, either sewn with their silk onto their host trees or fallen among the leaf litter beneath the trees.

□ **Habitat:** Emperors are present wherever there are hackberry, sugarberry and related trees. Both trees were once limited to floodplain forests and streamsides but have spread into most upland forests, hedgerows and other disturbed areas.

□ **Garden Habit:** Hackberry and Tawny Emperors are not avid flower nectarers and prefer overripe fruit or the sweat on your skin. Remember when they land on you that they also like to visit dung! They *do* visit some flowers (see nectar list) to nectar on, even though most references say otherwise.

□ **Garden Nectar Plants:** shrubs: butterfly bushes, rabbitbrush, dogwoods; perennials: milkweeds, rosinweed and cupplant; annuals: star thistle, *Verbena bonariensis*.

□ **Garden Host Plants:** large trees: hackberry and sugarber-

A Hackberry Emperor nectars on the honey-scented blossom of a butterfly bush.

Choose a hackberry (North), sugarberry (South) or both (middle of the continent) for your garden's shade tree(s). Netleaf or Lindheimer hackberry are small trees that are a good choice for Southwestern gardens. (You will host American Snout and Question Mark butterflies too.) Be sure to have a bed of shrubs, flowers or groundcover where fallen leaves can collect beneath your host trees, for the overwintering caterpillars to lie dormant in. The caterpillars crawl back up into the tree when the tree releafs in spring. A butterfly feeder of overripe fruit is a sure bet for attracting both emperor butterflies as well.

ry; small trees: Lindheimer, netleaf and dwarf hackberries.
□ **Identification:** The Hackberry Emperor (1.75 to 2.5 inches) and Tawny Emperor (2 to 2.75 inches) are small to medium-sized butterflies with very similar wing patterns. Emperors' outer forewings are speckled—white with one black eye spot on Hackberry, and orange with no black eye spot on Tawny Emperor. The hind wings have a similar row of black spots along the margin, with a wavy or zigzag line at the margin. In general, Hackberry Emperors are gray-brown and Tawny Emperors are brown-orange.
□ **Caterpillar:** The caterpillars feed in a herd and are green with two starry horns on their head. Emperors' Latin name means star (*aster*) caterpillar (*campa*). There are two broods of Hackberry Emperors and one brood of Tawny Emperors per year. The caterpillars of both species turn brown to overwinter. They may create a shelter of leaves attached together and to a twig with their silk, or their hibernation leaf may fall and they overwinter in the leaf litter beneath the tree.
□ **Chrysalis:** Their chrysalis is cryptic green and looks just like part of a hackberry or sugarberry leaf.

An orangish Tawny Emperor nectars on a butterfly bush.

Northern Pearly-Eye & Southern Pearly-Eye

Enodia anthedon and *Enodia portlandia*

Northern Pearly-Eye   Southern Pearly-Eye

Pearly-Eyes are denizens of the shady shadows of the forest's floor. They often land upside down on tree trunks to observe their domain and watch for passing mates. Their spots along the outer part of their wings are called ocelli and have a golden halo around each one. A pearly white cloud shrouds these spots on the butterfly's underside, which is how these butterflies got their name.

Pearly-Eyes are shy and seldom noticed by us, even though they are widespread and common in nearly any eastern woods. Get to know them and their subtle beauty! This goes for the other related butterflies in the satyr group, which includes the Little Wood Satyr, also found in woodlands, and the Common Wood-Nymph and Common Ringlet, which are denizens of open grassy spaces.

▫ **Status:** Pearly-Eyes are resident butterflies that overwinter as young caterpillars.

▫ **Habitat:** Northern Pearly-Eyes inhabit moist forests, woodlands or savannas and occasionally young, disturbed woodlands, as long as there is an understory with grasses intact. The Southern Pearly-Eye is associated with moist woodlands containing switchcane (our native wild bamboo), which usually grows in floodplains. Both species are never found away from trees.

▫ **Garden Habit:** Pearly-Eyes visit only shady woodland gardens with bunches of shade-loving grasses and natural plantings. Here males perch on tree trunks, and females search for grasses to lay eggs on. Both seek out nourishment from tree sap or will visit your butterfly feeder of overripe fruit.

A Southern Pearly-Eye displays an irregular row of spots on its forewing.

A Northern Pearly-Eye with its wings open. Note how the spots on the forewing line up in a row like beads on string.

▫ **Garden Nectar Plants:** Pearly-Eyes do not nectar on flowers but are avid visitors to butterfly feeders and prefer sap flows.

▫ **Garden Host Plants:** Southern: evergreen shrubs: switchcane and dwarf switchcane. Northern: variety of perennial grasses. The most gardenworthy are: bottlebrush grass and river oats.

▫ **Identification:** 2.25 to 2.75 inches. Pearly-Eyes are medium-sized woodland butterflies that are brown above and taupe colored below. They have a series of various-sized

The Gardener's Butterfly Book

Hang a butterfly feeder under a tree at the edge of a woods, and Pearly-Eyes are likely to visit. Leave wooded portions of the yard unmowed and plant shade-loving ornamentals and grasses like river oats and bottlebrush grass. Be sure to plant our evergreen native bamboo, called switchcane, in the South—it makes an effective woodland screen. Dwarf switchcane creates a great medium-height evergreen groundcover in shady areas.

spots along both wings. The spots are viewable from above and below but are more pronounced and colorful from below. Northern Pearly-Eyes' forewing eye spots all line up in a row like beads on a string, whereas Southern Pearly-Eyes' forewing spots line up on their edge toward the butterfly's body, giving the various-sized spots a curved-row look. It is amazing how similar two distinct species of butterflies can look to us!

❏ **Caterpillar and Chrysalis:** These are seldom seen and are cryptic green to blend in with their host plant, blades of grass leaves.

A Northern Pearly-Eye perched on a leaf in the forest understory. These truly are butterflies of the woods!

Little Wood Satyr

Megisto cymela

Every late spring, the woodlands of the eastern part of the continent come alive with the bouncy flight of the Little Wood Satyr. They emerge in numbers slowly at first but then appear in abundance—filling almost any woodland or forest edge. You can see how they received the mythical name of the god of the woods as their brief, bursting flights give them the appearance of revelry in the woods. Their mass appearance soon fades, as they have only one brood and will not be back again until the following year to repeat the performance.

Little Wood Satyrs seldom visit flowers—on occasion, they visit the stinky blooms of woodland edge shrubs like viburnums and, even more rarely, visit adjacent meadow flowers like the aromatic common milkweed. For food they prefer dung, tree sap or honeydew from aphid infestations.

▫ **Status:** Little Wood Satyr is a resident butterfly that overwinters as a young caterpillar.

▫ **Habitat:** Little Wood Satyrs are found in forest edges, woodlands, savannas and even young woods with rich grassy understories. They are found in these habitats in both rural and urban settings.

▫ **Garden Habit:** Little Wood Satyrs bounce in from adjacent woodlands, nearly oblivious to typical butterfly gardens.

The very similar Carolina Satyr is the southern counterpart to the Little Wood Satyr.

They are also uninterested in butterfly feeders filled with fruit. Little Wood Satyrs seldom stray far from the edge of the woods but become a resident of the naturalistic shade garden as long as there are uncut grasses present.

▫ **Garden Nectar Plants:** recorded at a few flowers: shrubs: dogwoods, sumacs, dewberries, viburnums; perennials: milkweeds, ox-eye daisy.

▫ **Garden Host Plants:** feeds on a wide variety of grasses, including the ubiquitous southern lawn grass, St. Augustine grass.

▫ **Identification:** 1.5 to 1.75 inches. A medium-small brown woodland butterfly with two eye spots on both the forewings and hind wings. These eye spots are visible from above and below.

A Little Wood Satyr shows off its flecks of shimmering wing scales found along the butterfly's underside row of spots.

Maintain natural woodland areas on your property and resist the temptation to mow brush. But remove exotic brush that often invades residential or woodlands near urban areas and shades out the wild grasses and mixed wildflower understory these butterflies need as habitat. Little Wood Satyrs seldom visit butterfly feeders.

□ **Caterpillar:** The miniature, boxy tan caterpillar is seldom noticed among the grass leaf blades.

□ **Chrysalis:** The small brown and slug-like caterpillar is seldom encountered—it looks like a brown leaf blade or leaf sheath.

□ **Local Relative:** Carolina Satyr (*Hermeuptychia sosybius*) is a similar satyr common in southern woodlands. The underside has a row of several eye spots and only one is pronounced on the forewing and two on the hind wing. It is plain brown above, with no eye spots. There are several related satyrs from around the country, most with quite limited occurrence.

A Little Wood Satyr basks on a leaf in its woodland understory habitat.

Common Wood-Nymph

Cercyonis pegala

The Common Wood-Nymph would be better named the meadow-nymph. It inhabits grassy meadows and only the sunny openings and edges of woods. This butterfly has an erratic, bounding flight, and it is difficult to observe until it lands. When they land, they reposition themselves in jerky jumps that seem to be in rhythm with their bounding flight. A perched Common Wood-Nymph may briefly snap open its wings as well—unless it is basking—when it holds its wings open to absorb the warm sunshine. When Wood-Nymphs are startled, they may fall into the grass or dart into dense shrubbery to hide.

Common Wood-Nymphs can become common in mid to late summer and really enliven a meadow. Their infrequent visits to the butterfly garden or butterfly feeder are a welcome sight. There are two distinctive color phases of the Common Wood-Nymph—more southerly populations have a striking yellow patch surrounding their forewing eye spots, while more northerly butterflies don't. We still don't know the "why" behind this difference in coloration.

▫ **Status:** Common Wood-Nymph is a resident butterfly that overwinters as a young, unfed caterpillar.

▫ **Habitat:** Common Wood-Nymphs inhabit treeless prairies, meadows, marshes and other grassy places. They are also found in openings in woodlands, savannas and grassy roadsides.

▫ **Garden Habit:** Wood-Nymphs bound into the garden to nectar on such non-native luxuries as butterfly bush and native flowers such as purple coneflowers and blazingstars. They seldom stay long before moving back to their meadowy habitat.

▫ **Garden Nectar Plants:** Wood-Nymphs readily visit but-

The southerly form of the Common Wood-Nymph has a yellowish patch surrounding its eye spots.

terfly feeders and occasionally nectar: shrubs: butterfly bush, buttonbush, rabbitbrush; woody vine: virgin's bower clematis; perennials: purple coneflowers, Joe-Pye-weed, wild geraniums, wild sunflowers, blazingstars, mountain mints, ironweeds, goldeneyes; biennial: thistles; annual: *Verbena bonariensis*.

▫ **Garden Host Plants:** many grasses including bluestems and purpletop.

▫ **Identification:** 1.75 to 3 inches. A medium-sized chocolate-colored butterfly that has dark scaling on its underside. On the forewing are two bold eye spots, which, in central and southern regions, have a yellow patch around them; in northern populations, these spots have only golden halos.

▫ **Caterpillar:** The pale-striped caterpillar is cryptic-green to match the grasses on which it feeds. It has a pair of reddish short tails on its rear end.

▫ **Chrysalis:** The chrysalis is green or yellow-green with paler mottlings and light edges to match the grass leaves on which it is formed.

A Common Wood-Nymph nectars on an ironweed blossom. This northerly form has no yellow patch surrounding its eye spots.

Place a butterfly feeder near a grassy meadow or over the flower border. If you have a large lawn, try to decrease its size and plant it with locally native meadow or prairie grasses and wildflowers. Like most butterflies, Wood-Nymphs like to nectar on butterfly bushes.

Local Relatives: There are three additional very similar, more restricted western species: Great Basin Wood-Nymph (*Cercyonis sthenele*), whose upper forewing eye spot is larger than the other spot below it, is found in California and intermountain regions in dry chaparral or dense woods. In California, it nectars on California buckeye. Mead's Wood-Nymph (*C. meadii*), with its orangy forewing wash, lives in dry ponderosa pine and sagebrush and nectars on rabbit-brush. Small Wood-Nymph (*C. oetus*) is the darkest species found in arid western habitats; it nectars on wild buckwheats.

A Common Wood-Nymph takes nectar from the blossoms of boneset.

Common Ringlet

Coenonympha tullia

The Common Ringlet is a butterfly on a mission—a mission to colonize the Northeast and Appalachian Mountains and boldly go where no ringlet has gone before (at least in historic times).

We tend to think of butterflies and their ranges as static but, actually, many are dynamic, and this is a good report of a positive change. About 1960, Common Ringlets spread from Ontario into the Northeast and, by 1994, reached southward into New Jersey. They continue their southward colonization—some butterfly authorities believe they will reach cool, mountainous north Georgia someday.

Common Ringlets vary in appearance from pale creamy or whitish brown among the golden grasses of California, to creamy yellowish to yellow-orange through the Rocky Mountains, to orange and brown into the northern prairies and northeastern meadows. They can be abundant in grassy areas, from outside Los Angeles to Seattle and eastward to New England cities—making the grasses sparkle with their flight as you flush them from their perches.

▫ **Status:** Common Ringlet is a resident butterfly that overwinters as a caterpillar. This butterfly is expanding its range in the Northeast as a resident butterfly (note that it is not a butterfly colonist—it stays year-round on its new turf).

▫ **Habitat:** Treeless prairies, meadows, marshes and other grasslands but also open grassy woods and even tundra.

▫ **Garden Habit:** Common Ringlets will venture into the garden as long as it is adjacent to their grassland habitat. They immediately go to yellow flowers in the composite family (asters, daisies, goldenrods, goldeneye, rabbitbrush) and alight to nectar.

▫ **Garden Nectar Plants:** shrub: rabbitbrush; perennials: marguerite daisies, coreopsis, gumweed, ox-eye daisy, goldenrods, goldeneye.

A Common Ringlet nectars on a white mustard.

▫ **Garden Host Plants:** miscellaneous grasses (it's not picky or host-specific as are many butterflies).

▫ **Identification:** 1.25 to 1.5 inches. You can only identify live butterflies by their underside while they nectar or rest. A lone eye spot in the upper corner (apex) of the forewing stands out, even though it is quite small in the pale California Ringlet. The orange wash in the forewing is a good field mark in eastern populations as well.

▫ **Caterpillar:** The caterpillar is seldom seen, camouflaged among the grasses—being dark green (or occasionally brown) with pale lateral stripes and a pair of short tails on its rear end.

▫ **Chrysalis:** Seldom encountered. Some of the regional variations are considered subspecies (ssp.) with Latin names. All were once known as different species: Northwest Ringlet (ssp. *ampelos*) of the Pacific Northwest, California Ringlet (ssp. *californica*) of Mediterranean California, Ochre Ringlet (ssp. *ochracea*) of the Rocky Mountains, Inornate Ringlet (ssp. *inornata*) of the prairies and Northeast.

The California race of the Common Ringlet is much paler and was once thought to be a separate species.

Grasslands, fields, meadows and other open but unsettled areas make necessary habitat. Don't cut grassy areas back, but let them grow. Most any grasses will do, as the ringlet isn't choosy as to which host plant it selects—only that it be a grass. Maintain a wild, grassy/weedy corner of your yard and don't let trees and shrubs invade. Plant yellow flowers too, for ringlets love yellow.

Monarch

Danuas plexippus

onarchs are clearly chief in the kingdom of butterflies. They courageously go where other butterflies wouldn't dare—they know they're toxic, so are pretty fearless, and their North American migration is extraordinary.

Monarch butterflies east of the Rocky Mountains winter in a few scattered, chilly mountains cloaked in oyamel fir, west of Mexico City. (There are a few stragglers on the mild lower Atlantic and Gulf Coasts.) Western Monarchs overwinter in groves of eucalyptus on the Pacific coastline of California or Baja California. In spring, the same southward-migrant Monarchs move northward—some all the way back to the middle of the country. New generations push far to the north and continue to colonize until the

A Monarch nectars on the bold autumn flower of a cosmos.

This female Monarch is laying eggs on a bloodflower milkweed.

threat of freezing weather sends their newly emerged off-spring on a southward migration they have never done before. In fall, they mass by the thousands, especially in sheltered sites near nectar-rich meadows or prairies or along geographic barriers like the Atlantic Ocean or the Great Lakes. A few get blown off course to England and southern Europe each year, but prior wayward Monarchs have successfully colonized Hawaii, New Zealand, Australia, Philippines, Indonesia and the Cape Verde Islands off Africa! Monarchs are also resident (nonmigratory) butter-flies of the West Indies, Central and South America.

A Monarch's toxicity is due to its host plant—milk-weeds—most of which contain a toxic alkaloid. The cater-pillar eats milkweed leaves and obtains the toxic compounds, which are retained through metamorphosis into the butterfly.

□ **Status:** Monarchs are our only true migrant butterfly: they migrate to wintering grounds, and the same butter-flies return, like many migrant birds, the following spring. Western butterflies overwinter in coastal California and Baja California. Eastern butterflies overwinter in montane forests of oyamel fir in central Mexi-co. The overwintering butter-flies are in effect refrigerated to lessen their metabolism and are in sexual diapause to also prolong their life. Migrant butterflies can live six months and reproduce on their northward migration. Reproductive summer Mon-archs do not live longer than one month. A few Monarchs are resident in south Florida.

□ **Habitat:** Monarchs inhabit all sorts of native and man-made habitats, from openings in forests and woodlands to marshes, prairies, meadows, fields, roadsides, yards and gardens.

□ **Garden Habit:** Spring Mon-archs returning from Mexico, or new southern generations moving north, need refueling during their long-distance flight. They stop to nectar and rest on nectar-rich spring flowers, and females will lay eggs on the first milkweeds they encounter. Monarchs readily complete their meta-morphosis on the garden's milkweeds and can defoliate plants. In fall, Monarchs bunch up to roost in sheltered trees adjacent to flower-filled

Walking through a cloud of Monarchs on their wintering ground in Mexico.

This Monarch has been tagged to track its annual migration to its wintering grounds in Mexico.

and clovers. Monarchs have quite a culinary palate!

❑ **Garden Host Plants:** Any species of milkweed (or a few odd, related plants in the same family). The weedy common and showy milkweeds have low amounts of the toxic alkaloid that the caterpillars ingest to become toxic. Plant other species to help the Monarch continue its distastefulness to warm-blooded predators. Monarchs are one of the few butterflies whose host and nectar plants are the same.

❑ **Identification:** 3.25 to 4.75 inches. A large black-margined and black-veined orange butterfly with brilliant white spotting along its margins—the classic warning coloration and pattern of toxic animals. The underside coloration is orange on the forewing and creamy tan on the hind wing—again with pronounced black wing veins. Only the Viceroy mimics this pattern but is usually smaller and has a black line just past the middle of the hind wing.

gardens. They congregate at flowers in fall to gain fat to fuel their long, arduous southward migration.

❑ **Garden Nectar Plants:** shrubs: groundsel-bush, butterfly bush (preferring the yellow-flowering cultivars), button-bush, lilacs (especially the later-flowering cultivars that are in bloom when it arrives from the South); vine: Carolina aster; perennials: milkweeds, asters, chrysanthemums, purple coneflowers, Joe-Pye-weeds, blazingstars, mountain mints, goldenrods (especially seaside, stiff and showy!); biennial: thistles; annuals: bloodflower, Spanish needles and bur marigolds, cosmos, lantanas, pentas, Mexican sunflower, zinnias; weedy plants such as dogbanes, mustards

❑ **Caterpillar:** Monarch caterpillars are a familiar sight on milkweeds and easy for budding naturalists to raise. (My mother always has a few milkweeds with accompanying Monarch caterpillars in the garden for the grandchildren to observe and learn about life.) They have two pairs of black, fleshy tentacles at each end and are striped white, yellow and black, again a warning coloration against predatory

Monarch caterpillars are a familiar sight on milkweeds. Their bright pattern acts as warning coloration to predators.

The Monarch chrysalis is decorated with droplets of gold. Here you can see the outline of the future butterfly's wing.

Plant several species of native milkweeds with staggered bloom times—in much of the East this includes purple milkweed, then butterflyweed and, finally, swamp milkweed. Bloodflower is a tropical milkweed you can grow as an annual in frosty zones—it blooms continuously and attracts Monarchs all summer. The Ajamete milkweed is a native shrubby milkweed for dry southwestern gardens and blooms over a long period of time. Avoid planting common and showy milkweeds, as they contain low amounts of the toxic alkaloid that protects Monarchs from predators. Plant late-summer and fall-blooming asters, blazingstars and seaside, showy or stiff goldenrods, which are all very important fall migration nectar sources.

birds and mammals.

▫ **Chrysalis:** The chrysalis is soft green with a black waist-band and studded with gold-like droplets. Simply radiant and extraordinary.

▫ **Local Relative:** Queen (*Danaus gilippus*) 3.25 to 3.75 inches. Queen is the more or less sedentary tropical cousin of the Monarch. Queens are orange-brown without black wing veins above but have the characteristic black margins and black veins on the underside. Queens are resident butterflies that fly all year in frost-free parts of the Southwest and Florida, where they far outnumber Monarchs in summer. They colonize and stray northward in the south Atlantic states and the southern Great Plains. Their host and nectar plants are the same as Monarchs'. Their caterpillar has bright yellow bands in its wider black bands and has three pairs of fleshy tentacles (two extra in the middle). Queen's chrysalis is nearly identical to the Monarch but smaller and often pinkish white instead of pale green.

Queens are the non-migratory, southern counterpart to the Monarch.

SKIPPERS

Skippers are unique, mostly little butterflies that have bent-antennae clubs and thick bodies with strong wing muscles. Because of their wide bodies, their wings appear shorter in proportion. Many gardeners think skippers are moths and ignore them. The following pages show those skippers you are apt to have in your garden throughout most of the country. Basic identification is discussed but even the experts cannot be sure which species some of them are, without dissecting them in the lab. You can learn to identify most of them, but don't worry if you make a mistake. The butterfly police won't come and arrest you—they will just give you an award for welcoming, observing and enjoying these feisty little denizens of our gardens. Skippers' bulbous-headed caterpillars are all quite similar. Skippers become a chrysalis (pupate) unattached to any support, in a loosely woven, cocoon-like place that the caterpillar created by sewing leaves together.

Silver-Spotted Skipper
Epargyreus clarus

The Silver-Spotted Skipper's name suits it, both in English and Latin. The hind wing's silver spot is clearly visible as the butterfly visits the garden and this spot is the butterfly's most identifiable feature. The genus *Epargyreus* part of the Latin name is Greek for "silver," and the species name *clarus* means "clarity." Incidentally, the silver spot is on the underside of the wing, and the butterflies never rest with their wings open, so the silver spot is always in view, even though this butterfly is in the subfamily of skippers known as spread-wing skippers. The other spread-wing skippers rest with their wings fully outspread. There is a mustard-gold splotch on the forewing, but this identical spot is shared by one of its more localized cousins, the Hoary Edge (described below).

Silver-Spotted Skippers are big, rugged skippers and may visit the garden on days too dreary for others. They are completely at home in the garden and may nectar all around the yard and create a new generation on your wis-

A Silver-Spotted Skipper nectars on sedum.

trees and wisteria vines.

❑ **Garden Habit:** Silver-Spotted Skippers are nectar lovers, so commonly inhabit flowery gardens, where they incessantly skip from flower to flower. They nectar from a wide array of plants but only from flowers with the following hues: pinks, lavenders, purples and blues. They may lower their color standards to yellow mustard flowers in spring or fall, when nectar sources are limited.

❑ **Garden Nectar Plants:** shrubs: butterfly bush, buttonbush, late-flowering garden lilacs; perennials: milkweeds, wood mints, blazingstars, bergamots; vine: morning glories; biennial: thistles; annuals: balsam impatiens, annual vinca, salvias, zinnias; weedy plants: dogbanes, clovers and vetches.

❑ **Garden Host Plants:** shade tree: black locust and its hybrids and cultivars; small trees: New Mexican locust, rose acacia; shrub: indigobushes; woody vine: wisterias, especially American wisteria.

❑ **Identification:** 2 to 2.5 inches. This widespread and common butterfly is the easiest skipper for beginners to identi-

The easily identified Long-Tailed Skipper is a Silver-Spotted Skipper relative found in southern gardens.

teria vine or locust tree. You may get unhappy with them on your native American wisteria vines—they can completely tie up and disfigure the foliage. The caterpillars make great fishing bait if you need to control them.

❑ **Status:** Silver-Spotted Skipper is a resident butterfly that overwinters as a mature caterpillar or as a pupa.

❑ **Habitat:** Silver-Spotted Skippers reside in woodland and forest openings and edges and in urban areas with locust

The dark, bulbous head of the Silver-Spotted Skipper's caterpillar is typical of all skippers.

The Gardener's Butterfly Book

and green body. They live in nests of folded leaves pulled together with their silk. The folded leaf nests make them easy for gardeners to locate. They can be pesky on your favorite wisteria vine.

▫ **Chrysalis:** The caterpillar forms a brown pupa in its leaf nest.

▫ **Local Relatives:** Hoary Edge (*Achalarus lyciades*) is more limited in range and garden visitation, as it prefers more wild areas. It has the same forewing spot but does not have the silver spot; it has a scaly whitish edge to its hind wing, so it is aptly named as well.

Long-Tailed Skippers (*Urbanus proteus*) are another largish close cousin of the Silver-Spotted Skipper and readily visit gardens in the deep South. They are unmistakable, with their long hind wing tails and their beautiful wash of iridescent greens and blues.

fy! The large size (for a skipper) and metallic, silvery white spot centered on the hind wing make it unmistakable.

▫ **Caterpillar:** The caterpillars have a bulbous dark head

The Silver-Spotted Skipper is well named and one of the easiest skippers to identify.

Skippers

Northern Cloudywing & Southern Cloudywing

Thorybes pylades and *Thorybes bathyllus*

Northern
Cloudywing

Southern
Cloudywing

The Northern and Southern names for these two cloudywings are somewhat of a misnomer. This is because the Northern Cloudywing is found far to the north—well into Canada—but is *also* found well to the south of the Southern Cloudywing, in Florida and into Mexico. Southern Cloudywing is found only in the hot-summer areas of eastern North America and was once called the Eastern Cloudywing; it has expanded its range northward in recent years. The more ubiquitous Northern Cloudywing was once called just Cloudywing, as it is the most widespread and common cloudywing in North America.

Cloudywings have one early summer flight in the North but have more broods into fall in the South. They don't

A Northern Cloudywing perched on an acacia with its wings closed, looks very moth-like.

have brilliant colors but enliven a woodland or woodland-edge garden, where both may be present in much of eastern North America.

▫ **Status:** Cloudywings are resident butterflies that overwinter as fully grown caterpillars.

▫ **Habitat:** Cloudywings are always found in open woods or woodland edges. They can be found in urban areas where the woodlands are not too immaculately maintained or where weedy exotic honeysuckles, privets and buckthorn brush have not been allowed to choke out the entire understory.

▫ **Garden Habit:** Cloudywings usually just skip through the garden—just passing through, looking for a mate or host plant. They will briefly stop to nectar on their favorite flowers. Just like the Silver-Spotted Skipper, they are partial to white, pink, violet or blue flowers! They can reside in large gardens with open woodlands that are unmown.

▫ **Garden Nectar Plants:** shrubs: butterfly bushes, buttonbush; perennial: milkweeds; annual: *Verbena bonariensis*; weedy plants: dogbanes, clovers, vetches.

▫ **Garden Host Plants:** The caterpillars feed on lots of wild pea family plants including milk-vetches, bush-clovers, tick-trefoil, clovers and vetches. Round-headed bush-clover is the most gardenworthy and is available from nurseries specializing in prairie wildflowers.

▫ **Identification:** 1.25 to 1.75 inches. Cloudywings are pretty much evenly golden brown with a few speckles on their forewing. Southern Cloudywing has pronounced white

Northern Cloudywing has only tiny white speckles on its forewing.

Maintain any woodland area you own by removing invasive exotic shrubs like honeysuckles, privets and buckthorns, which shade out the weedy wild pea plants (and all other wildflowers) that these and many other butterflies need to have for their caterpillars to feed on. Plant a drift of *Verbena bonariensis* and milkweeds—two plants they can't resist to stop and nectar upon—to draw them from wildlands into your garden.

speckles—an hourglass-shaped one at the mid-forewing margin is usually distinct. Northern Cloudywings have less pronounced speckling but the two species can be quite similar. If you have close-focusing binoculars, you'll notice that Southern Cloudywings have a white face, while Northern Cloudywings are golden brown.

❑ **Local Relative:** Confused Cloudywing (*Thorybes confusis*) can be just as common in your garden if you live in the Southeast. It confuses the easy identification between Northern and Southern elsewhere—it has small forewing speckling and a white face!

The larger speckles on the forewing help identify this basking Southern Cloudywing.

Hayhurst's Scallopwing

Staphylus hayhurstii

The name of this tiny butterfly has finally been standardized by the North American Butterfly Association. Old references will show it as "Southern Sooty-Wing" or "Scalloped Sooty-Wing." Both its common and Latin names are after Dr. L. K. Hayhurst of Sedalia, Missouri (an -ii at the end of Latin species name is the equivalent of a possessive apostrophe). Mr. Hayhurst was the first to describe the butterfly's life history and sent his description to the great butterfly expert, W. H. Edwards, who named the butterfly after Mr. Hayhurst in 1870.

The scallopwing name comes from the angular wings that have a lovely fringe on their outer edges. The fringe color alternates, taupe and dark black, which accentuates the wavy wing edge look. This pattern is more distinct in female butterflies. Hayhurst's Scallopwing is found in late spring into summer and nearly all year except midwinter in Florida. The presence of this tiny butterfly in the garden is much celebrated because of its refined and unique beauty.

□ **Status:** Hayhurst's Scallopwing is a resident butterfly that

Sweet-smelling heliotrope is the key to attracting tiny, beautiful scallopwings.

Hayhurst's Scallopwing at rest.

TIPS
TO ATTRACT

Plant a border of single orange marigolds with complementary blue sweet-smelling heliotrope. Double marigolds have fewer or no nectar-filled disk florets (the miniature flowers in the center of daisy-like flowers) for the butterflies to feed from. Heliotrope is also called cherry pie plant, because it smells like cherry pie (or vanilla or baby powder). Be sure to smell the plant's flowers before you purchase them, because some varieties lack the wonderful scent. Heliotrope is actually a tropical shrub and can be overwintered indoors in a sun-filled window.

overwinters as a caterpillar.
- **Habitat:** The butterflies favor disturbed open woods or woodland edges.
- **Garden Habit:** Hayhurst's Scallopwings relentlessly nectar with their wings outspread, mostly on their two favorite flowering garden plants: marigolds and heliotrope.
- **Garden Nectar Plants:** annuals: heliotrope, marigolds, verbenas; weedy plants: dogbanes, clovers, mints.
- **Garden Host Plants:** weedy plants: lamb's quarters, Joseph's coat.
- **Identification:** 1 to 1.25 inches. The only tiny, nearly black spread-wing skipper with scalloped-edged wings found in much of the country. If you look really close, you will notice their smattering of gray hairs (wing scales). Females have more of these contrasting scales, so are a bit more dramatically colored and patterned.

The typical view of a Hayhurst's Scallopwing with its wings locked in an outspread position.

Skippers

Gallery of Duskywings

Duskywings are small (not tiny) blackish brown skippers that nectar with their wings spread wide open. The species are quite similar to one another but the four described here are the ones you are most likely to encounter in your gardens in most of the country.

▫ **Status:** Most Duskywings are resident species overwintering as caterpillars. Funereal Duskywing overwinters only in mild parts of the Southwest and colonizes north and eastward in summer.

▫ **Habitat:** varies—see species accounts.

▫ **Garden Habit:** Duskywings are enticed by the recommended flowers into gardens to nectar. Unfortunately, they seldom stay for any length of time. They also like to sip moisture from puddles.

▫ **Garden Nectar Plants:** small trees: redbud, wild plums; shrubs: buttonbush, blackberries, garden lilacs; perennials: Joe-Pye-weeds, mountain mints, goldenrods; annuals: globe amaranth, *Verbena bonariensis*; weedy plants: winter cress, dogbane, mints, clovers.

▫ **Garden Host Plants:** varies—see species accounts.

▫ **Caterpillar:** Duskywing caterpillars fold leaves over or together and tie them together with their silk to create a nest.

▫ **Related Species:** There are several additional duskywing species found in various ranges throughout the continent, but they do not readily visit gardens or are limited in distribution.

JUVENAL'S DUSKYWING

Erynnis juvenalis (1.5 to 2 inches)

Juvenal's Duskywing has only one brood per season, so the butterflies are only found in springtime and only near oak woodlands or naturalistic parks with groves of oak where there are seedling and sapling trees. Invasive exotic shrubs

A Juvenal's Duskywing perched on a leaf.

threaten this butterfly's woodland understory home, just as with the cloudywings and many other butterflies. Juvenal's Duskywing gets its name from Juvenal, the first-century Roman satirical poet. The old name for the butterfly is "Eastern Oak Duskywing," which accurately describes the butterfly's habitat.

HORACE'S DUSKYWING

Erynnis horatius (1.75 to 2 inches)

Horace's Duskywing is the duskywing most at home in the average garden, provided small oaks are planted or allowed to grow in unmaintained areas in the neighborhood. It is unknown whether its ancient Roman namesake Horatius was the legendary hero or the poet. Horace's Duskywings have multiple broods, so are present from early summer to fall.

The Horace's Duskywing is the most frequently encountered duskywing in gardens.

WILD INDIGO DUSKYWING

Erynnis baptisiae (1.5 to 1.75 inches)

Wild Indigo Duskywing is a butterfly that has adapted to our degraded landscape by acquiring a new taste in host plants. They are the namesake of wild indigos, which were originally its primary host. Highway departments introduced a new pesky plant called crown vetch to protect highway cuts from eroding. Wild Indigo Duskywings have changed their host to crown vetch and have greatly

TIPS
TO ATTRACT

Plant a border of mixed-colored globe amaranths back-dropped by a tall stand of *Verbena bonariensis* to attract summer and fall-season duskywings. Allow white clover in your lawn to attract early-season Juvenal's Duskywing into your yard.

increased in numbers, as has the crown vetch, which is willy-nilly wreaking havoc on native wildflowers as it smothers them out. If you want Wild Indigo Duskywings, plant native wild indigos. Blue wild indigo is a long-lived popular garden perennial. Dispose of any crown vetch on your property as it will inadvertently wreck the habitat for other butterflies. Wild Indigo Duskywings are present from early summer to fall.

Spreading dogbane, a native prairie plant that duskywings love.

Wild Indigo Duskywing.

FUNEREAL DUSKYWING

Erynnis funeralis (1.25 to 1.75 inches)

The Funereal Duskywing is one of the easiest of the dusky-wings to identify. It's named for its black garb with a brilliant white-fringed edge to the hind wing. (As in the outfit one would wear to a funeral.) The contrasting white fringe on the hind wings can be seen from afar. Funereal Dusky-wing is a southwestern species but readily colonizes the lower Midwest and western South in summer. Hayfields are a boon to its expansion, as alfalfa is a major host plant. In the Southwest, plant a New Mexican locust tree as a host plant.

A Funereal Duskywing nectaring on coreopsis.

Common Checkered-Skipper

Pyrgus communis

The name Common Checkered-Skipper describes this butterfly well. This tiny, white, spread-wing skipper with an overlaid gray checkered pattern is common and widespread. This butterfly inhabits gardens all year in frost-free or nearly frost-free zones and is found in summer and fall northward, becoming a colonist or an irregular colonist at the northern edge of its range. Some butterfly experts consider this butterfly to be the most common species of skipper.

Common Checkered-Skipper is one of the easiest skippers to identify in gardens across most of the continent. Only its related species confuse identification in peripheral regions of the continent. These skippers are pugnacious and territorial in the garden among their chosen turf of favorite nectar plants. They will dart out and investigate

This White Checkered-Skipper is nearly identical to the Common Checkered-Skipper but is found in Southwestern deserts.

passing butterflies or other moving objects, both animate and inanimate.

▫ **Status:** Common Checkered-Skipper is a semi-hardy resident butterfly overwintering as a caterpillar in mild-winter regions. After mild winters, the butterfly colonizes regions far to the north in summer. The butterfly is in flight all year in frost-free regions.

▫ **Habitat:** Common Checkered-Skippers inhabit all types of open disturbed habitats, including yards and gardens.

▫ **Garden Habit:** Common Checkered-Skippers are more than just brief visitors—they can live their whole life in the garden. They will metamorphosize on their garden host plants, nectar on the recommended nectar plants, court, mate and lay eggs once again in the garden.

▫ **Garden Nectar Plants:** perennials: asters, chrysanthemums, mistflower; annuals: Spanish needles, globe amaranth, marigolds, *Verbena bonariensis*, Mexican zinnias; weedy plants: fleabanes and clovers.

▫ **Identification:** 1.25 to 1.5 inches. The only white skipper with the checkered gray pattern in most of the country. (See relatives species, below.)

▫ **Garden Host Plants:** perennials: hollyhocks, poppy mallows, globe mallows and copper mallow; biennials/annuals: mallows; weedy plants: most weeds in the mallow family.

▫ **Local Relatives:** There are several nearly identical and challenging-to-differentiate checkered-skippers—mostly found in peripheral or pristine habitats. Tropical Checkered-Skipper (*P. oileus*) is a common garden visitor in semitropical gardens and is nearly identical to Common Checkered-Skipper. White Checkered-Skipper (*Pyrgus albescens*) is frequent in suburban gardens, where it replaces the Common Checkered-

A Common Checkered-Skipper perched on an alfalfa blossom.

TIPS
TO ATTRACT

Plant any of the screaming magenta-flowered poppy mallows as host plants with tall blue *Verbena bonariensis* and contrasting orange single marigolds for nectar. This beautiful and award-winning composition is sure to attract Checkered-Skippers and many other butterflies as well.

Skipper in the hot deserts of the Southwest. Two-Banded Checkered-Skipper (*P. ruralis*) is found in Pacific Northwest and northern Rocky Mountain meadows and hillsides. The Grizzled (Checkered) Skipper (*Pyrgus centaureae*) is widespread in cool regions. In alpine country, Grizzled Skippers are present every other year (odd years), because it takes two seasons in these frigid, short-summer environments for them to complete their metamorphosis.

A Common Checkered-Skipper spreads its wings to show how it got its name.

Common Sooty-Wing

Pholisora catullus

The tiny Common Sooty-Wing resides across the country in edge habitat such as roadsides. An old name for the butterfly is the "Roadside Rambler." Common Sooty-Wing is widespread and has sooty black wings, so its new name is most appropriate too. A brassy sheen across the outer portion of all four wings and a few tiny, sharply contrasting bright white dots near the forewing apex make it easy to identify—there are even a few noticeable white spots on its head. The butterfly rambles along edge habitats, fencerows and lot lines to visit gardens, where it nectars with its wings wide open. The butterfly seldom visits for long before moving on.

▫ **Status:** Common Sooty-Wing is a semi-hardy resident butterfly that survives milder winters and overwinters as a mature caterpillar; it colonizes northward every year.

▫ **Habitat:** Common Sooty-Wings are common in any type of disturbed habitat from woodland edges, yards and gardens, meadows, old fields and roadsides.

▫ **Garden Habit:** Common Sooty-Wings visit the garden to nectar or puddle but usually move on unless you have their host plants in the garden.

Ironweeds, like this Missouri ironweed, are favored Common Sooty-Wing nectar sources.

This top view shows how the Common Sooty-Wing got its name.

Plant annual cockscomb for a beautiful, non-weedy caterpillar host, and plant or allow white clover to complement your lawn for nectaring. In late summer, Common Sooty-Wings favor the nectar of purple sprays of New York ironweed or other tall ironweed. These nectar sources bring the butterfly up to eye level for you to closely observe. Be sure to leave host plants intact through the winter, or place them in piles where the hibernating caterpillars will not be crushed.

□ **Garden Nectar Plants:** vines: gourds and melons; perennials: milkweeds, ironweeds; annuals: globe amaranth, *Verbena bonariensis* and other verbenas; weedy plants: dogbanes, mints and clovers.

□ **Garden Host Plants:** annuals: celosias or cockscombs, summer poinsettia; weedy plants: lamb's quarters, amaranths/pigweeds.

□ **Identification:** 1 to 1.25 inches. This is the only tiny, spread-wing skipper with evenly sooty black wings. The most similar butterfly would be the Hayhurst's Scallop-Wing, which is not as dark and has scalloped wing edges.

□ **Caterpillars:** They are seldom seen but roll leaves or tie leaves together with their silk to create nests. They overwinter in these nests.

A Common Sooty-Wing basks on gravel. It does not perch with its wings locked outspread like its close relative the Hayhurst's Scallopwing.

Gallery of Grass Skippers

The tiny grass skippers are named for their host plants—various species of grasses. They are easy to identify as a group by their stout wings and large bodies. They often look like a triangular wedge when they nectar, but they also bask and nectar with their forewings partially spread open and their hind wings completely open, giving them a paper airplane look.

Grass Skippers are present in every garden—often abundant in late summer and fall—and greatly increase the life and beauty of a butterfly garden. Embrace their subtle beauty and get to know them!

❏ **Status:** The grass skippers are resident butterflies whose caterpillars overwinter in their nest of silken-tied grass leaves.

❏ **Habitat:** These grass skippers are the species found in open woods, meadows, yards and gardens.

❏ **Garden Habit:** Hardy grass skippers can spend their whole lives in the garden, especially if you have some unmaintained grassy border or ornamental grasses planted in your garden.

❏ **Garden Nectar Plants:** shrubs, perennials, biennials and annuals. See "Tips to Attract" on page 199.

❏ **Garden Host Plants:** lawn and weedy grasses, some ornamental grasses.

❏ **Identification:** 1 to 1.25 inches. A good way for beginners to learn to identify the grass skippers is to learn them by their underside, which is all you really see clearly when they visit your garden.

❏ **Caterpillar:** Grass skippers' caterpillars are tiny and seldom seen. They have large, bulbous heads and long, fat bodies and roll grass blades together with silk to create a protective nest.

❏ **Chrysalis:** They pupate in the caterpillar's leaf nest.

ZABULON SKIPPER
Poanes zabulon

Other names for this skipper are "Southern Golden Skipper" or "Southern Dimorphic Skipper." Zabulon Skippers are very territorial and take up residence, with a favorite perch in the garden.

A male Zabulon Skipper nectaring on lantana.

PECK'S SKIPPER
Polites peckius

Also called "Yellow Patch Skipper," this skipper is easily identified by being golden brown with an irregular pale yellow patch on the hind wing and can be abundant in gardens.

A Peck's Skipper on a Depthford pink.

DUN SKIPPER
Euphyes vestris

Also called the "Sedge Witch," this "grass" skipper's caterpillars feed on sedges and not grasses.

A Dun Skipper.

TAWNY-EDGED SKIPPER
Polites themistocles

The Tawny-Edged Skipper is best identified by its even, bronzy gold coloration and tawny tan fringe on the edge of its wings—perfectly named! A bit of orange is visible from the base of the forewing.

A Tawny-Edged Skipper nectaring on a flower.

LEAST SKIPPER
Ancyloxypha numitor

Least Skippers are most common near grassy swales, creeks, rivers and marshes. They have a slower flight than the other skippers and are evenly golden orange below and dark above.

A Least Skipper.

EUROPEAN SKIPPER
Thymelicus lineola

European Skipper was introduced to London, Ontario, around 1910, British Columbia in 1960 and Colorado in

A European Skipper nectaring on red clover.

1985—the Ontario escapees have now spread throughout northeastern North America and all are still expanding their range. European Skippers are golden orange with a lighter wing fringe and have very short antennae.

DELAWARE SKIPPER
Anatrytone logan

Delaware Skippers prefer moist, disturbed areas, including yards and gardens. They are bright yellow-orange, so look like a wedge of cheddar cheese with no other markings. There are several similar species, but they are restricted to native habitat.

A Delaware Skipper perches on an eryngium.

TIPS
TO ATTRACT

Plant ornamental grasses in your garden as host plants for grass skippers. Wild or any cultivar of rose verbena and garden lilacs are great nectar sources for the spring species. *Verbena bonariensis* and single marigolds are possibly their favorite summer and pre-freeze nectar sources. Be sure to plant some fall-hardy flowering plants like single asters ('Jenny' is most nectar rich), single chrysanthemums ('Sheffield Pink' is a superior cultivar) or frost-tough verbenas ('Tamari Burgundy' is nectar rich). All these flowers bloom in Indian summer after a frost, when the grass skippers are still at their peak of garden abundance.

Gallery of Western Grass Skippers

Six grass skippers are widespread solely in the western mountains and readily visit flower gardens. They nectar on: shrub: rabbitbrush; perennials: asters, blazingstars; biennial: thistles; annual: frogfruit.

ORANGE SKIPPERLING

Copaeodes aurantiaca (1 inch)

Orange Skipperlings are fast-flying skippers with a pointed head. They inhabit grasslands and woodlands near washes, streamsides and other wetlands, just like the Least Skipper. They are golden, plain yellow-orange at rest with their wings closed. Orange Skipperlings emigrate into the northern Southwest and southern Great Plains.

An Orange Skipperling nectaring.

WESTERN BRANDED SKIPPER

Hesperia colorado (0.75 to 1.25 inches)

Western Branded Skippers are a highly variable olive golden or reddish orange with white speckles both on their fore and hind wings. The outer hind wing spots form the shape of a comma or chevron. They were once called the "Comma Skipper" for this mark. The butterflies are found in mid to late summer in grasslands, alpine meadows and brushlands.

A Western Branded Skipper nectaring on gumweed.

JUBA SKIPPER

Hesperia juba (1 to 1.5 inches)

Juba Skippers prefer drier chaparral, open and pine or juniper woodlands and sagebrush brushlands. They are similar to the Western Branded Skipper but are darker

A Juba Skipper nectars on rabbitbrush.

greenish bronze and the hind wings are more translucent. An old name, "Jagged-Border Skipper," refers to the jagged band of white spots on the hind wing. The butterflies are found from spring until fall.

SANDHILL SKIPPER

Polites sabuleti (0.75 to 1.25 inches)

Sandhill Skipper is a tawny skipper whose hind wing has an irregular yellow spot and yellow veining. This butterfly resides in moist meadows, alkali (salt) grasslands (which is how it gets its old name "Saltgrass Skipper") and yards, where it feeds on lawn grasses. Sandhill Skipper is expanding its range eastward.

Sandhill Skipper.

UMBER SKIPPER

Poanes melane (1.25 inches)

Umber Skipper was once found only in southern California but has expanded its range throughout Mediterranean California. Umber Skippers have reddish brown hind wings with vague yellow spots. They nectar on shrubby abelias, Jupiter's beard and thistles found in suburban yards and

grassy wastelands. Mainly a butterfly of western Mexico, they also inhabit the Big Bend of Texas and colonize southeastern Arizona.

Umber Skipper perched on a blade of grass.

WOODLAND SKIPPER

Ochlodes sylvanoides (0.75 to 1.25 inches)

Woodland Skipper was once called the "Western Skipper," as it ranges throughout much of the nondesert West. The butterfly is bronzy gold with angular yellow or creamish spots on the hind wing. It inhabits country like that of the Juba Skipper and has only one flight in summer. It is slow flying and remains in the same area all its life, readily nectaring on flowers throughout the garden.

A Woodland Skipper nectaring on wild asters.

Emigrant Grass Skippers

Several species of grass skippers are residents of the deep South or semitropics and annually spread northward in summer. The very nature of their preference for disturbed open habitats allows them to be quite at home in yards and gardens. The Sachem and Fiery Skipper colonize most of the country by late summer and become abundant in gardens with marigolds. Their caterpillars feed on lawn grasses, and they become common even in northern gardens by Indian summer.

A Fiery Skipper shows its golden wings flecked with a few dark spots.

SACHEM

Atalopedes campestris (1.25 to 1.5 inches)

Sachems have a marbly golden brown and golden pattern, and the females are quite large, deeper golden brown with pale yellow marbling forming an outward-pointing crescent on the hind wing.

A Sachem nectars on a zinnia.

FIERY SKIPPER

Hylephila phyleus (1.25 to 1.5 inches)

Fiery Skippers are golden orange with a few dark spots. Turf-care professionals considered Fiery Skippers pests in manicured lawns. They become abundant in late summer gardens. Fiery Skippers were introduced to Hawaii, where they now reside on all the major islands.

WHIRLABOUT

Polites vibex (1.25 to 1.5 inches)

Male Whirlabouts look much like Fiery Skippers, but their hind wings have four distinctive larger dark spots. Females are dull olive gray-brown. Whirlabouts seldom (but on occasion) colonize anywhere beyond the American South, where they're abundant in gardens along with the Fiery Skipper and Sachem—together, they are known as the "three wizards."

A Whirlabout nectars on Spanish needles.

EUFALA SKIPPER

Lerodea eufala (1.25 to 1.5 inches)

The Eufala Skipper was formerly called the "Gray Skipper," for obvious reasons—this skipper is pale bronzy gray beneath, with rather indistinct lighter spots upon close inspection.

A Eufala Skipper on a wild verbena.

OCOLA SKIPPER

Panaquina ocola (1.25 to 1.5 inches)

Ocola Skippers were actually named after the Ocala Indians who once resided in the Ocala, Florida region. They have dark brown, long, narrow forewings, which project well beyond the hind wings, and they were once known as the Long-Wing Skipper. Newly emerged butterflies have a beautiful violet sheen. Ocola Skippers move en masse both northward in summer and southward in fall but are not true migrants.

An Ocola Skipper with its beautiful, violet-sheened wings.

CLOUDED SKIPPER

Lerema accius (1.25 to 1.75 inches)

Clouded Skippers are black grass skippers that look much like the female Zabulon Skipper but lack the white hind wing edge. Its white forewing apex spots differentiate it from Dun Skipper. Clouded Skippers colonize the southern half of the continent and have a very long proboscis, so can nectar on long-tubed flowers like impatiens.

A Clouded Skipper nectars on Spanish needles.

BRAZILIAN SKIPPER

Calpodes ethlius (2 to 2.25 inches)

Brazilian Skipper is also known as the Canna Skipper, and its caterpillar can be a pest on these ornamental flowers. The caterpillar is uniquely transparent, and you can see its heart and other internal organs. Brazilian Skippers emigrate up coastal areas and the Mississippi Valley, following their host plant from garden to garden. Brazilian Skippers are relatively large with long, reddish bronze-colored wings that have several translucent spots visible on both wings when the butterfly nectars or rests. The huge increase in popularity of cannas may propel this butterfly even farther north in summer.

A nectaring Brazilian Skipper.

Gallery of Roadside-Skippers

Roadside-Skippers are tiny skippers that are mainly black or dark brown with gray dusting—they are often called the dusted skippers. These butterflies are technically in the grass skipper subfamily and can be nearly impossible to differentiate from each other when their wings are old and worn. There are many more species in the genus but the others are more localized or habitat restricted to undisturbed woodlands and rare in yards and gardens. Most of the rarer southeastern species' including the beautiful Lace-Wing Roadside-Skipper (*Amblyscirtes aesculapius*) host plant is the native wild bamboo, called switchcane. Do them a favor and plant a cane thicket if you live near wildlands. The more prevalent species prefer edge habitat, which is exactly what a road creates and, hence, their common name.

▢ **Status:** Roadside-Skippers are resident butterflies that overwinter as a caterpillar.

▢ **Habitat:** Roadside-Skippers inhabit open wooded and brushy edge habitats. They will venture into yards on occasion, especially the Celia's and Nysa Roadside-Skippers.

▢ **Garden Habit:** Roadside-Skippers are usually just brief visitors to the garden as they move along wooded corridors and hedgerows.

▢ **Garden Nectar Plants:** perennials: rose verbena, vervains; annuals: marigolds, *Verbena bonariensis* and other verbenas; weedy plant: selfheal.

▢ **Garden Host Plants:** weedy grass: gardenworthy; semi-perennial: river oats.

▢ **Identification:** 1 to 1.25 inches. Roadside-Skippers look somewhat like Sooty-Wings or Scallopwings (both spread-wing skippers) but are technically grass skippers and perch with their wings closed. They bask a bit differently than the other grass skippers and hold their forewings only partially open and nearly perpendicular to their outspread hind wings. As with the grass skippers, all identification concerns the butterfly's underside.

NYSA ROADSIDE-SKIPPER
Amblyscirtes nysa

This Roadside-Skipper is especially fond of yards and gardens in the Southwest and southern Great Plains. It is easily distinguished by its marbled hind wing.

COMMON ROADSIDE-SKIPPER
Amblyscirtes vialis

The term "common" is a misnomer, as this roadside-skipper is uncommon and really just the most widespread species. It will visit the garden if you live near brushy edge habitat. This skipper is similarly patterned to the Common Sooty-Wing but doesn't hold its wings outspread, and has the characteristic dusting to the outer edge of its forewing and most of the hind wing.

A Common Roadside-Skipper perched on a blade of grass.

A Nysa Roadside-Skipper.

Celia's Roadside-Skipper and Bell's Roadside-Skipper are apt to visit yards and gardens and are almost impossible to tell apart; they were once considered the same species. They are black with dusting and a few tiny white speckles on the hind wing. Bronze Roadside-Skipper (*Amblyscirtes aenus*) is a southwestern species.

The Bronze Roadside-Skipper is a citizen of the American Southwest.

INDEX